DOORWAYS
WOMEN, HOMELESSN
TRAUMA AND RESIST/
Photographs, Essays, In

CW00509316

BEKKI PERRIMAN

Featuring contributions by
LAURA E. FISCHER, ANDREA GIBBONS,
JANNA GRAHAM, PIPPA HOCKTON,
ANNA MINTON, MARY PATERSON,
MOYRA PERALTA, LISA RAFTERY,
SHIRI SHALMY and
ANDREA LUKA ZIMMERMAN

with an afterword by KATE TEMPEST

For Arna

CONTENTS

FOREWORD

FOREWORD
MOYRA PERALTA

Where would we be without our artists? They touch the soul. And disturb our complacency.

Bekki Perriman is one such. The vision behind her Doorways Project, riveting in its authenticity, captures our attention completely. And in a world that habitually tries to avert its gaze, her sound recordings from homeless individuals further serve to ensnare and enlighten us — if we but open our hearts. John Berger called this 'recognition': the ability to hear another person's reality.

The reality of being deliberately excluded. A serious phrase to contemplate, so damning and prevalent within humanity. Bekki treads carefully in presenting her considerable knowledge and her direct experience of the mostly hidden face of Britain. But where is the furious groundswell of protest from the rest of us at the sheer unacceptability of rough sleeping and homelessness in our 'civilised' society?

I urge you to consider the dedication and the message underlying Bekki's work in this book, honed as it is by her own understanding.

Whilst our elected representatives have paid little heed for the past ninety years or so to those excluded within our disparate society, we NEED the voices of our artists, now more than ever, to refocus our thinking on the continuing crimes against humanity.

As a kindred spirit and photographer, it was my great pleasure to meet Bekki for a short time in 2015, and acquaint myself with her valuable work ... I entreat you to do the same.

DOORWAYS
BEKKI PERRIMAN

I used to sleep here. It was sheltered and tucked away.
I've noticed they have now put a massive flowerpot
in this space to keep the homeless out.

BEKKI PERRIMAN

This is the doorway where Andy and I used to sleep.
In this doorway we had water thrown on us by the street
cleaners. We were spat on, urinated on and threatened
so many times. In this doorway we also found friendship,
shared a cup of tea and cuddled up together to keep
warm. We laughed into the night.

DOORWAYS

BEKKI PERRIMAN

In this doorway a man came and whispered in my ear
that he 'wanted my money' and showed me a knife
he had in his hand. I gave him the few pounds I had
made selling *The Big Issue*, absolutely terrified. Attacks
like this are so common on the streets it didn't occur
to me to tell the police.

DOORWAYS

BEKKI PERRIMAN

I was sleeping rough in this doorway. An off-duty social worker came and approached me. She promised me she would come back the next day and help me to get some help. The next day I waited over twelve hours desperate for her to return as she had promised. But I never saw her again.

DOORWAYS

BEKKI PERRIMAN

I sold a *Big Issue* here to Chris Evans.

BEKKI PERRIMAN

Andy and I built ourselves a little cardboard house
on these steps. It was a childlike house with a cut-out
window and flap-open door. We sat inside our soggy
house in the pouring rain. A man who walked past went
across the road and bought us a pizza. I remember
sitting inside our little cardboard house eating pizza
as one of the happiest days on the streets.

DOORWAYS

BEKKI PERRIMAN

In this doorway the police used to always move
me on, but they never told me where I could go.

DOORWAYS

BEKKI PERRIMAN

My friend Maria and I used to sleep in this doorway.
A religious group would drive up in their multi-coloured
van and try and persuade us to go and live with them
on their farm. One evening Maria left with them. She
was expected to give up her sexuality (she was lesbian),
convert to their religion, hand over her giro and give
them all of her possessions. She was eighteen years old
and had been sleeping rough for a long time. Although
she felt trapped living with their rules, they gave her
a home and so she stayed with them, but it was at such
a high cost.

DOORWAYS

BEKKI PERRIMAN

Andy was unconscious on the steps. I was shaking him, but he was lifeless and blue. Crowds of people were coming out of the opera and I begged them to call an ambulance. A few people stopped and stared but then continued on their way. I still cannot comprehend how so many people could walk past a seventeen-year-old boy dying in a doorway.

DOORWAYS

BEKKI PERRIMAN

THE DOORWAYS
PROJECT
BEKKI PERRIMAN

The Doorways Project was inspired by my experiences as a young woman on the street. It began as a photography project, photographing the doorways where I used to sleep. I wanted to tell the stories of those doorways as a way of expressing the invisibility and horror of homelessness, but also as a way in to telling stories of friendship and everyday life. Most people walking along those streets, past the doorways in my photographs, will be going shopping, wandering around casually on a day out, or going to the theatre. But those streets were my home for many years.

While the public may understand the multitude of reasons why someone can end up homeless—such as relationship break-down, the loss of a job, bereavement, domestic violence, childhood abuse, leaving prison, care or the army, substance misuse or mental ill-health—very few people understand the reality of living on the streets.[1]

Sometimes it feels like every street in the West End holds a memory, and I know those streets intimately. I know the side alleys, the short cuts and the places to hide. I know where there are heating vents blowing out hot air, offering a warm space to bed down. I know where the shops leave out discarded food in bin bags, sandwiches still protected by plastic and good to eat. The rhythm of the early hours: the street cleaners on their machines hosing down the steps; being woken up by building owners who move you on. How to get a free sleeping bag. The day centre for showers, lockers and a hot breakfast.

The wounds that are invisible are the hardest ones to heal. Those are the streets where I sat for hours and was verbally abused by members of the public almost every day just because I was homeless. Those streets hold memories of repeated trauma: being sexually assaulted, beaten up, spat and urinated on. Incidents of violence became part of the fabric of street life.

Every day was just about survival. This has been echoed by many of the people I've met sleeping rough: 'Once you are on the street every day is just a survival experience and if you go to bed and you wake up the next day without bruises then you know you have really survived that day.'[2]

However, the street was also the place where I found friendship, family and a sense of community deeper, more loyal and intense than I have ever known since. We looked out for each other and protected one another; though despite that, it was never really safe. I was one of those people who would have been described as 'entrenched' homeless, or 'chaotic', because I kept going back. I'd stay in a hostel or a squat for a few weeks and

BEKKI PERRIMAN

then end up back out on the street again. Sleeping rough had a magnetic pull and there was something about the homeless culture that kept me there. There were a number of factors. Friendship was a big part of it, and a sense of belonging. I didn't know it at the time, but I was also struggling with severe mental health problems and complex Post-traumatic Stress Disorder (PTSD). I felt safer outside. Sleeping rough was brutal but staying in hostels often felt more unsafe.

The Doorways Project, of which this book is a part, starts from an embodied experience of homelessness. As an extension of the photography series of the doorways where I once slept, the project became a touring, site-specific sound installation, exploring homeless culture through the personal stories of society's most silenced people. I interviewed people across the country — in Glasgow, Edinburgh, London, Brighton and Liverpool — who were currently or had recently been sleeping rough. The recordings of the interviews were edited into a series of short monologues installed in city centre doorways.

The intention of the work was to catch an accidental audience, people walking past who would never usually stop and listen to someone who is homeless. The audiences were invited to intimately engage with the difficult (and mostly ignored) experience of homelessness and to hear first-hand the challenges it presents. It created a unique opportunity to observe a familiar environment from a different perspective.

The doorways were carefully chosen to replicate sleeping spaces, though we ensured that the locations were not actually an individual's sleeping space as we did not want to displace anybody. While choosing locations I was looking for spaces I might once have chosen to sleep in — recessed doorways such as fire exits and loading bays; doorways with heating vents blowing out hot air; doorways that are covered, sheltered and surrounded by three walls to block out the wind.

By offering homeless people a voice and bringing those voices to city centre locations, we were aiming to humanise a situation that many people find threatening and uncomfortable, and to challenge notions of blame and victimisation. The direct voice, apart from asserting its human presence, enables listeners to connect on a personal level and to enter the speaker's world of experience.

The causes of homelessness are often complex, and it is a social issue that is widely misunderstood. Public attitude surveys

THE DOORWAYS PROJECT

suggest that one of the biggest misconceptions is that people living on the streets are there by choice, founded on an assumption that issues such as mental health, substance misuse, debt or relationship breakdown are the fault of the person concerned.[3] But homelessness is rarely a choice and prior to becoming homeless people do everything they can to prevent themselves ending up on the streets. Yet it has been recognised by those working with the homeless that people sleeping rough for a period of time 'acclimatise' to the streets and become part of homeless culture.[4]

The majority of the people I interviewed had been on the street for a long time and I was particularly interested in exploring the concept of 'entrenched' homelessness. When I arrived in Brighton the first person I met was a street drinker called Tom (not his real name). He told me: 'I know I am going to die on the streets. I've been on the streets twenty-five years. I stayed in a shelter last night and I can't cope with four walls. The way I am going, with my drinking, I will pickle my liver, that is what will kill me. But I'd rather die on the street than go inside again.'

It can feel like living on the streets is full of contradictions. The street is both a place where there is a feeling of community and belonging, and a place that is so frightening and full of danger. People I spoke to described very similar experiences to mine, where friendships on the street were part of the culture, and they talked about other homeless people as family, using terms like 'sister' or 'brother' to describe the closeness of their relationships (see Interview with Arna, p. 46). However, every person I interviewed also talked about how dangerous being on the streets is and all had experienced verbal abuse from members of the public.

One of the aims of this book is to specifically address and try to understand the experiences of homeless women, who form one of the most marginalised groups in society. There are complex reasons why women find themselves on the street and most street-homeless women have experienced multiple traumas. Women on the streets are the minority, but every single woman I interviewed for The Doorways Project told me about experiences of sexual harassment while being street homeless, and many had been raped or sexually assaulted, as you will read in the transcripts included here. They experienced repeated harassment from the public and especially from men who assumed that because they were sleeping rough they would sell themselves for sex.

Every woman I interviewed had difficulty accessing housing support and many described themselves being passed in circles from one agency to another and back again, with no one willing to take responsibility. Many services are not equipped to deal with complex trauma and don't know how to support women with multiple needs. A report published by St Mungo's in 2014, 'Rebuilding Shattered Lives', discusses how women with a dual diagnosis of substance misuse and mental health problems are excluded from services as their difficulties are considered too complex.

This resonates with my personal experience. When I was homeless I was told by the Homeless Person's Unit that I wasn't 'in priority need' as I didn't meet their criteria for risk or vulnerability. But when I tried to access emergency hostels I was turned away as my needs were assessed to be 'too high' for low-support accommodation. It didn't make sense; the council were saying I wasn't 'vulnerable enough' to be housed but I was repeatedly turned away from emergency hostels for being 'too vulnerable'.

When you are on the street it is difficult to find help or protection from the authorities. I've spoken to homeless young people who have tried to access benefits but have been told they need to prove they are 'estranged' from their family. The job centre asks them for a letter proving estrangement; but how do you get this letter if you have left difficult and unsafe family circumstances? This is exactly what happened to me too.

Many women on the streets are mothers who have had their children taken away from them:

> As with most parents, women who are homeless care deeply for their children, but often their situation — especially the complexity of their needs and unresolved trauma — means they are separated from their children; some lose custody of their children permanently. Homelessness itself can be a key factor. A specialist outreach worker from Street Talk noted that 'in my experience, women's housing situations are used against them when it comes to custody of children. Social services frequently use "having no appropriate housing" as a reason why children should be removed'.[5]

Tracy, whose interview is included in this book, talks about having a daughter who was adopted while she was on the street. She describes feeling like they were waiting for her to fail. In the end, it was not her addiction that meant her daughter was taken from her, but the very fact that she was homeless.

THE DOORWAYS PROJECT

The situation of homelessness is so dehumanising that you start to feel separated from mainstream society. This separation or sense of 'us and them' runs so deep that it becomes hard to understand or empathise with another person's reality. Some of the responses I had to The Doorways Project were very telling about the way homeless people are perceived. For example, the comments section below a feature about the project in the *Brighton Argus* was full of angry responses to the work:

> This whole situation just gets worse and now we have someone providing the lifestyle choice as a piece of entertainment. I have no idea what the council are doing to eradicate these drink and drug fuelled types, although maybe a good starting point would be to remove the piles of debris and detritus that they accumulate and prosecute everyone they find begging.[6]

Likewise, despite commissioning the project, at times it was hard to work with cultural organisations as some didn't understand the piece. At one venue the security guard commented to me when I was standing in the fire exit that this 'wasn't art and it was just encouraging homelessness'. He would constantly hose down the doorway where the work was installed, making it a wet and uncomfortable place to stand. His reasoning for the constant hosing down of the doorways was that he didn't want anyone to beg there. In other venues there were repeated problems with the sound not being turned on and the MP3 boxes were in rooms we weren't allowed access to, so we couldn't turn on the sound ourselves. It felt like a metaphor for what I'd experienced on the street: the parallel of the hosing down of the steps where I once slept and having my work silenced by some of those who had the power, the same way I was often silenced while homeless.

I found it really difficult as an artist, as people had trusted me to tell their stories. I felt a lot of responsibility in representing their narrative and I kept the stories true to how they were spoken. The subjects of the interviews were often disturbing and difficult to hear. One person talked about losing friends to suicide, alcohol addiction and murder; another woman talked about being raped on the streets. If a story was challenging, or made audiences feel uncomfortable, I felt it was crucial in communicating what the situation is really like for people on the street. The stories offered a window into what people's lives are like. People sharing their memories with honesty, emotion, humour, warmth or anger humanised the experience of homelessness.

BEKKI PERRIMAN

We had many positive responses to the work, often acknowledging its power to move and unsettle and to transform perceptions. When I went back to Brighton I met a homeless man who was standing listening to the work. He said to me: 'I stop and listen to her story every day, because her experiences [of heroin addiction] are so much like mine and it comforts me to hear it.'

There were times making the work when I just wanted to give up. It felt too difficult, and I was finding it hard to cope with what I was witnessing on the street. I was listening to people knowing that they were going back to sleep in a doorway and feeling so guilty that I couldn't do anything to help make their housing situation better. At the same time I was being drawn back into my own traumatic memories, which I'd worked so hard to bury. One afternoon I was doing the install for the exhibition at Metal in Liverpool, when Red (one of the people I interviewed) rang. He was calling me to tell me that Tom had died. I remembered that first time speaking to Tom and how he'd said to me he knew he was going to die on the streets. I was on the platform of Edge Hill station, tears streaming down my face, hanging photographs of the doorways where I had once slept and feeling so completely overwhelmed by the rawness of it all.

The Doorways Project started as an artistic intervention to challenge the existing notions around homelessness. As it has developed and grown it has raised many questions. Street homelessness is so complex and there is so much to try and understand; I'm not sure an art project can do justice to the complexity of the situation. It also raises questions about art. Who is it for? What do the people taking part get from it? People were happy to share their stories and they wanted others to know about their experiences. Most of the people who took part came back and listened to the work. They invited people they knew to hear it and told their customers they sold *The Big Issue* to, or members of the public, to go and listen. But was playing their stories in city centre doorways empowering or was it too exposing? Whatever the answer to these questions, to understand street homelessness we must listen to homeless people and to their individual stories. I hope that The Doorways Project will not only give voice to the plight of those who are systemically unheard, but that it will also show their humanity.

My experience in making The Doorways Project has been that many people with no direct personal experience of homelessness have already made a judgement about people on the streets.

THE DOORWAYS PROJECT

The things I regularly hear are: 'They are just choosing to be there,' 'They'll spend all their money on drugs,' or the sympathy element, 'But I'd take drugs too if I was in their situation,' and so on. Everybody has made a judgement, and perhaps this is the only situation in which every single day someone abuses you, just because you are sitting in a doorway. To be abused every day just because you don't have somewhere to live leaves a mark.

I leave you with a piece of writing called 'Your Eyes of Hostility', which I wrote on the back of a leaflet when I was eighteen years old and already knew the streets intimately. It was 1996 and the writing was published in *The Big Issue*.

YOUR EYES OF HOSTILITY

What gives you the right to look at me and judge me? You don't know me, I have never done anything to hurt or upset you. I am not standing in your way. Why do your eyes show so much hostility? I might be homeless, but I am a person too. I am not asking you for anything, just offered you a smile when your eyes met mine and in return all you do is glare. I wish the ground would swallow me up as you mutter under your breath and curse me. I sit in this doorway with society's rejects and you dressed in your suit and tie, money jingling in your pockets, throw insults spit and curse. Do you realise the kind of pain you put me through? And how much you make me hate myself? The scars on my arms always heal, inside it takes so much longer. So many of you pass me by every day and make assumptions about the sort of person I am. You blame me for my situation and never stop to ask why.

1 MEGAN RAVENHILL, *The Culture of Homelessness* (Hampshire: Ashgate Publishing Ltd., 2008).
2 Interview with Red, The Doorways Project, Brighton (2016).
3 NICHOLAS MILLS, *The Political Construction of Homeless Identities: Discourse and Contested Definitions of Homelessness*, PhD Thesis (Leicester: De Montfort University, 2005), available at uk.bl.ethos.414933.
4 RAVENHILL, *The Culture of Homelessness*.
5 SARAH HUTCHINSON, ANNA PAGE and ESTHER SAMPLE, 'Rebuilding Shattered Lives: The Final Report' (2014), available at http://rebuildingshatteredlives.org.
6 'Project Highlighting the Plight of the Homeless Launches for Brighton Festival', *Brighton Argus* (25 May 2016), comment.

BEKKI PERRIMAN

THE REAL HOUSING CRISIS
AND HOW WE OVERCOME IT
ANDREA GIBBONS

We live in a world awash with the rhetoric of housing crisis, but what we are seeing is a system that is working. It is working to produce massive profits, which does not mean the same thing as producing the homes so desperately needed.

Crisis resides instead in the suffering of each and every human being without a home. Each life so reduced (yet never fully reduced, because every human life is always a thing of wonder and potential) is further pared down by the rising numbers that make lived suffering abstract. Numbers that grow beyond our capacity to make sense of them. Too often, to be homeless means to be violently categorised as a thing among other things, a situation instead of a person: a statistic. Each figure sitting beside their cup, asleep on the street, or moving from couch to couch with nowhere to call home, is injury embodied. Yet to be one of tens or hundreds—forget the tens of thousands—makes empathy difficult. Enumeration renders those counted as less than human. Scale anaesthetises against both outrage and empathy. Being daily in the presence of such numbers also renders those of us who are housed as less than human, as we too often feel we can only turn away. It is in our power to respond to, support, offer help to one human being in need. But ten? Twenty? A thousand? How hard not to shut down in the face of such suffering where you cannot possibly help everyone?

Yet scale matters, if only to underscore that the roots of such suffering lie not in individual failings but in structural injustice. In 2010, when the Tory-Lib Dem coalition government took power, the number of people without homes was at an historic low. The implementation of austerity changed everything, cutting budgets and stripping away the limited safety net buffering the impact of the neoliberal policies of Blair's Labour government. The number of people accepted as homeless by councils rose steadily to 58,000 in England alone by 2016, despite redefinitions of duty and the introduction of a local residence requirement in order to lower the number of people councils must accept and thus produce a lower count.[1] The number of people reduced to rough sleeping has more than doubled, and current estimates stand at 34,500 people in England over the course of a year.[2] An average of 170 evictions took place per day—more than 60,000 a year—in the UK in 2015, part of a huge spike from the 5,000 people made homeless after being evicted from private rented housing in 2010 to 18,000 in 2016. This new flood swells the steady flow of those separating from partners when things just don't work out, teenagers leaving home under difficult

ANDREA GIBBONS

circumstances, people fleeing abusive relationships, those who have lost their jobs or finally given way beneath debt, and those fighting addiction and alcoholism with ever fewer places to seek support, particularly for the mental health issues that are frequently an underlying cause.

Such circumstances might cause temporary homelessness in any housing system until people find their feet. The lack of long-term, genuinely affordable housing is the main driver of the explosion of both the numbers finding themselves without a home, of the amount of time they are forced to survive in such a way, and whether or not in the end they do survive it on the streets. It is believed that in 2016 at least 3.34 million people took refuge with friends and family, a 'hidden' homelessness causing stress and overcrowding. Those seeking help and being placed in temporary accommodation increased by 52 per cent between 2011 and 2016, yet funding has steadily fallen and hostels have closed. In 2015–16 there was an estimated shortfall of 16,692 spaces.[3] Many do not find the help they need at all. The use of B&Bs has increased by 250 per cent since 2010, at extraordinary cost to both those being housed there as well as to councils. Privatisation allows private landlords to profit on human need while policy prevents councils from investing those millions in housing to replace all that has been lost under the right to buy. In London, where rising rents, regeneration and gentrification have hit hardest, a leaked 2015 government document stated that local councils had moved over 50,000 families out of the city entirely because they could not find them suitable housing provision. Many more tenants were being moved from the centre to the outskirts in a process widely understood by the community as social and ethnic cleansing. Most councils have thrown up their hands and implemented Tory policy without putting up a fight; there even seems to be some enthusiasm from certain Labour councils.[4]

We are in a crisis of housing provision, if not of profit. Yet still our government not only refuses to build social housing on any meaningful scale, but actively tears it down. Over 1 million people are registered on waiting lists; more than 20,000 people wait endlessly on each of several London boroughs' lists. Over 35,000 people in England have been waiting on these lists for more than ten years (since devolution, Wales and Scotland no longer keep records of such figures).[5] This is the result of policy, massive subsidies and incentives put towards promoting home ownership for decades, accelerating under Thatcher as an ideological project of creating a nation of homeowners rather than council tenants and maintaining its trajectory through Labour and Conservative governments.[6] Yet spiralling house prices make it impossible for younger people to get onto the housing ladder (if that is any longer their desire), leading to the ubiquity of 'generation rent'. Increasingly, people live with strangers, filling flatshares and the so-called Houses in Multiple Occupation (HMOs) with their private rooms and shared spaces. It works for some; for others the tensions are almost unbearable.

Luxury housing continues to be built. Anyone who has been in a town or city in the UK has seen the giant cranes looming over the centre. They sit crouched above the rubble of buildings coming down, the intimate glimpses of wallpaper and plumbing suddenly naked before wrecking balls finish their work to fill lots with nothing but bricks and twisted metal. In a world of shrinking resources and climate change, we witness the destruction of solid public buildings and council homes so proudly built over the past sixty years, and capable of standing at least another sixty despite years of budget cuts and managed decline. We witness the building from scratch of housing no one actually needs, in shiny metal and synthetic materials mined and fabricated and then transported long distances; buildings that will require immense ongoing resources to cool and heat and light and maintain—the height of mad unsustainability. The contradiction lies not just in the fact that much of the housing being torn down is both sound and well-loved, as demonstrated by the many campaigns that have sprung up to save it, but that its destruction is being sold to the public as a housing solution, despite the fact that more 'affordable' housing is being destroyed than is being built.[7] Affordability itself has been redefined as a percentage of median rents rather than a percentage of people's income, cynically tied to inflated markets rather than take-home wages or benefits. The underlying argument for such policies is that building any kind of housing to expand supply will solve this crisis. Economists have reached some agreement on this as a self-serving fallacy, borne out by ample experience— yet it continues.[8]

There is a logic at work here, clearly, but one of increasing profit rather than of providing for social need. On the one side stands the post-war consensus around healthy and decent housing as a right for all residents of Britain, to be provided by their government and funded through progressive general taxation. The decades of austerity after the Second World War saw this vision built in brick and concrete, with the construction of social housing on a massive scale. War's end offered the opportunity for a deeper

ANDREA GIBBONS

integration of society itself through such building schemes, and council housing was developed in the wealthiest of neighbourhoods where bombs had ripped through the material fabric of social and economic hierarchies. In living memory Britain attempted to build its way to a more just and equal society. Until Thatcher.

Since then we have been privatising and building ourselves out of it.

Those on the other side, now ascendant, see housing only as a commodity — something to be bought and sold, an investment, a source of profit rather than a home. To become such a commodity all regulations on a property and all sense of it as a home must be violently stripped away. This means actively seeking to erase housing regulations and move housing from public to private ownership. The desires of tenants and local communities are both considered irrelevant to this process of financial gain. Grenfell looms as a skeletal and sickening reminder of just where social tenants stand in this world we have created, those residents who survived the flames still scattered and living in tenuous and unsuitable accommodation. Aditya Chakrabortty sums up what can be learned from government's response to so many dead, lost to a lack of regulation and a greedy cutting of corners: absolute contempt.[9]

Such contempt both springs from and feeds the relationship between the belief in the market ideal and the desire for profit. The past few decades have seen real estate take the place of manufacturing as the great economic driver. Experts call this 'financialisation', where housing has become a security or financial instrument traded on the global market to generate billions in abstracted paper money. In such a process, housing is no longer understood primarily as a place to live or even to collect rent from, but as an asset that earns money by being bought or traded or held, as land values are driven up through speculation. Property often *loses* value through the complicating presence of a tenant.[10]

The ground for this has been prepared over decades by neoliberal policies changing the structures of housing and financial markets across the world through deregulation of corporations, the erasure of planning, development and banking constraints, and restrictions on protest. New regulations work to make government accountable to investors and corporate interests rather than citizens. This helps explain why it is impossible for a resident to purchase a single home in many new developments in cities such as London, Cardiff or Manchester, even as local governments claim

THE REAL HOUSING CRISIS AND
HOW WE OVERCOME IT

them as victories for housing development. They are only sold as a bundle of units, marketed directly to investors in Hong Kong or Singapore. These investors thousands of miles away constitute the 'public' that both the developer and architect have in mind in designing the buildings' use and aesthetic. In effect, and in the words of the UN's Special Rapporteur on Housing, financialisation 'refers to the way housing and financial markets are oblivious to people and communities, and the role housing plays in their well-being'.[11]

This bubble economy has been supported and subsidised by the UK government, which has argued that it is necessary for economic recovery from the 2008 crisis caused by... the bubble housing economy. Global housing investors have shown their ability to thrive and profit from crisis, whose cost they push onto the poor through policies of austerity, even as they buy up masses of foreclosures, offer cash for assets at a fraction of their worth and channel the profits out of communities and into offshore banks.[12] Many local councils in the UK have enthusiastically embraced the steady sell-off of social housing as a way to compensate for austerity's slashing of their budgets, becoming a key part of the massive transfer of wealth from the poor and working classes to the already rich.

To make this possible in a nation that once believed in housing for all has required the destruction of the consensus around housing as a right. This has been in motion since Thatcher's 'Right to Buy' policies in the 1980s, though in many ways it is increasingly reaching backwards into history to Victorian notions of the deserving and undeserving poor, blaming the poor for their own poverty rather than global housing markets, low wages and high unemployment, and the increasingly prohibitive costs of food, housing, heat, transportation and childcare. A steady discourse has issued from both government and media demonising those on welfare, justifying a punitive regime of humiliating punishments and sanctions to reduce welfare budgets, despite growing need. Tory policy has stripped young people of housing benefits, while for others they have been capped, leading to debt and eviction.[13] Food banks are giving out millions of parcels; thousands of deaths have been attributed to fuel poverty; rates of suicide and mortality are rising and can be tied directly to austerity policies.[14]

On the one side, respect for each other as human beings and the belief that everyone should have a safe, secure, decent home; on the other, the prioritisation of making a profit on housing with no thought for those who have none. The choice seems easy.

ANDREA GIBBONS

In her report to the UN, the Housing Rapporteur describes some solutions: 'a full range of taxation, regulatory and planning measures in order to re-establish housing as a social good, promote an inclusive housing system and prevent speculation and excessive accumulation of wealth.'[15] We have to cut through the complexities of financialisation, get to the fact that ultimately we need to decide what kind of world this will be, and join the struggle to make it so. These injustices were created by human beings, which means we can dismantle them, repurpose and build the homes we need, build the world we need.

1 All of these figures, except where otherwise indicated, are from SUZANNE FITZPATRICK et al., 'The Homelessness Monitor: England 2017' (2017), available at www.crisis.org.uk/media/236823/homelessness_monitor_england_2017.pdf. For reductions in service see also DAWN FOSTER, 'Why Council Waiting Lists Are Shrinking, Despite More People in Need of Homes', *The Guardian* (12 May 2016), available at www.theguardian.com.
2 KIRSTEEN PATON and VICKIE COOPER, 'Domicide, Eviction and Repossession', in *The Violence of Austerity*, ed. Vickie Cooper and David Whyte (Northampton: Pluto Press, 2017), pp. 164–70; Centre for Social Justice, 'Housing First: Housing-led Solutions to Rough Sleeping and Homelessness' (2017), available at www.centreforsocialjustice.org.uk.
3 MARK GOLDUP, 'Report to National Housing Federation—Strengthening the Case: The Cost Consequences' (2017), available at http://s3-eu-west-1.amazonaws.com/pub.housing.org.uk/Sitra_Strengthening_the_Case_for_Supported_Housing_(2017)_Full_Report.pdf.
4 MATTHEW TAYLOR, '"Vast Social Cleansing" Pushes Tens of Thousands of Families out of London', *The Guardian* (28 August 2015), available at www.theguardian.com.
5 FOSTER, 'Why Council Waiting Lists Are Shrinking'.
6 DANNY DORLING, *All That Is Solid: How the Great Housing Disaster Defines Our Times, and What We Can Do About It* (Milton Keynes: Penguin Books, 2015).

7 Ibid.; PAUL WATT and ANNA MINTON, 'London's Housing Crisis and Its Activisms', *City*, 20:2 (2016), pp. 204–21, available at www.tandfonline.com/doi/pdf/10.1080/13604813.2016.1151707.
8 Dorling, *All That Is Solid*.
9 ADITYA CHAKRABORTTY, 'How Power Operates in Modern Britain: With Absolute Contempt', *The Guardian* (3 July 2017), available at www.theguardian.com.
10 STUART HODKINSON and GLYN ROBBINS, 'The Return of Class War Conservatism? Housing Under the UK Coalition Government', *Critical Social Policy*, 33:1 (15 October 2012), pp. 57–77; UN Human Rights Council, 'Report of the Special Rapporteur on Adequate Housing' (Geneva: UN, 18 January 2017), pp. 17–770, available at https://digitallibrary.un.org/record/861179/files/A_HRC_34_51-EN.pdf.
11 Ibid.
12 Ibid.
13 Shelter, 'Shut Out: Households Put at Risk of Homelessness by the Housing Benefit Freeze' (June 2017), available at http://england.shelter.org.uk/__data/assets/pdf_file/0005/1391675/LHA_analysis_note_FINAL.pdf.
14 DANNY DORLING, 'Austerity and Mortality', in *The Violence of Austerity*, pp. 44–50; J. PRING, 'Welfare Reforms and the Attack on Disabled People', ibid., pp. 35–43.
15 UN Human Rights Council, 'Report of the Special Rapporteur on Adequate Housing' (1 March 2017), p. 21.

ANDREA GIBBONS

← Z

1
•
WHERE I SLEPT
LAST NIGHT:
Under the
Golden Jubilee Bridge

BEKKI PERRIMAN

Arna

I came to the women's refuge as I'd been battered by my previous
partner and it wasn't safe for me to stay in the area. After leaving
the refuge I got together with the wrong guy. I knew he was violent
and had a criminal history, but I fancied him, and it was the biggest
mistake of my life. I got involved with heroin and became an addict.
I went to jail, lost my flat when I was in jail and so I came out with
nothing. It was literally just doorways and parks.

It was scary, really scary. I actually lost my voice. I had laryngitis,
I think, and so I couldn't speak and I had no voice at all. Some guy
tried to get into my sleeping bag with me and I was at the taxi rank
and I said to him, 'If you don't go I'm going to start screaming,'
but where I couldn't scream, I couldn't make any sound and I was
literally sat there and shouting 'Help!' and no noise was coming
out and that was probably the lowest point for me, cos I just felt
so vulnerable and he could have done anything.

Drunk people thinking it's ok to use me as a bathroom, I hated that,
and I was sleeping with one eye open. You don't get proper sleep
because you are uncomfortable, you are on the hard floor and you
are looking out expecting someone to come and abuse you. Late
at night when the pubs were kicking out, you would get groups of men
that would find it funny to abuse a homeless person, so you would
be on your guard and you would try and find somewhere to sleep
where they wouldn't find you.

I got offered money so often to have sex with people, which I'm
sure they wouldn't do to a man, but because I was a woman, they
assumed I was a slut and that was offensive. I felt pretty degraded
already, being on the street, and to have someone say 'I'll give you
fifty quid' makes you feel like you are nothing, you are just a body
to be used. I never did it, but I know girls that have.

I always described being homeless as a balloon. When it's full and
inflated, it floats, and when it's deflated it sinks and then you get
a pin and stab it just to make sure that it is dead, that is the way
I felt—like that helium balloon which is deflated and being stabbed.
I hate even remembering it to be honest.

INTERVIEW

I went to the night shelter and they didn't take women at the time so they gave me an orange plastic sheet to keep warm and I thought, 'I'm a woman on my own on the streets and you are giving me an orange plastic sheet, which is going to make me even more obvious to everyone walking by,' and I just found that totally ridiculous and very unhelpful.

I'd get up really early, about 5 a.m., go to the toilets, use the bathroom, have a wash, clean my teeth, brush my hair and then I'd go and sit at the long benches and wait for someone to turn up. I'd probably start drinking about 10 o'clock in the morning and I'd drink all through the day. I also did get a heroin habit again because I just needed to numb it. At about 8 or 9 o'clock at night I'd go and find some cardboard, sometimes I would go to the back of the hotel and pinch some covers, and I'd go and sleep in a doorway by the taxi rank.

After two months of that we slept in a tent in the cemetery and every single day the council would come and tell us to go and we'd just move the tent 10 feet across. But it was horrific, it was really horrible. I woke up one morning dreaming I was swimming the channel and I'd actually woken up in a puddle, where it had rained so much, and it sort of congregated in the bottom of the tent. But I woke up thinking I was swimming the channel, that is how real it was to me.

We would look for places to sleep where there wouldn't be too much wind. When there is wind and rain together you get drenched and it takes ages to dry out. When we were broke we'd go somewhere where people will see us, because hopefully they will give you some money. But the main thing was keeping dry and warm, so we'd go to subways under the road and sleep in bushes and shop doorways that had big porches.

When I first ended up on the streets I was completely clean, I was sober. But the days are so long, sitting around doing nothing, and you feel everything, and you don't want to because it hurts, so my way of not hurting was to drink and to take heroin. It stopped me feeling and it also meant I could actually sleep at night, because without that I wasn't sleeping, I was too scared. I drank and I used heroin to make myself not feel and to sleep.

I know a lot of people say, 'I won't give homeless people money because they'll go and spend it on drink and drugs.' But I wasn't a drinker or a drug user until I became homeless. I became a drinker

Arna

and a drug user because I was homeless; I wasn't those things before. It was just to cope, because it is really tough. It hurts; physically and emotionally it hurts. Silly things, like if you can't find cardboard to lie on, your hips hurt because you are lying on the concrete and it's a proper physical pain and you can't sleep through physical pain. A lack of sleep is soul destroying; it just makes you feel so down. I totally sympathise with people who say 'I'm a drug user,' because I've been homeless, because that's what I was and I wasn't before.

I don't think I could have got much lower to be honest. I was in the pits of despair, for want of a better way of putting it. I just felt like there was no tomorrow and if tomorrow did come it was going to be as bad as today and I just didn't want to face that.

Most people walking past just ignored me and I became very adept at being invisible. I hated being invisible; I loathed it. I didn't matter to anyone and I'd try and make conversation with people, but they would be so stand-offish and back away from me, it was horrid.

The support services were dreadful. There was nothing. A rough sleepers service arranged for me to get onto a script to stop me from using, but apart from that, there was nothing. I just had an orange plastic sheet. I went to the council and they were like, 'Come back in three weeks,' and I said, 'What am I supposed to do for three weeks?' They said, 'Go and stay with a friend,' but I didn't have friends who had places of their own.

It was the other people on the street that were the ones who made me feel safe and protected me. I honestly think the other street people are the best human beings in the world. I have so much respect for them. If it wasn't for them, I probably wouldn't be alive to be honest. You become like a family. Thinking about one person in particular, a guy called Dave. He has been street homeless for about four years and he knew I was sleeping on my own. One night he was like, 'I'm not letting you stay on your own, I'm going to stay with you,' and I was thinking, 'Oh he wants something,' being a bloke and all that. But he didn't, he actually stayed up all night watching over me and he gave me his sleeping bag and he became my brother through it. I do, I call him my brother, even though we are not actually related, he is my brother in the true sense of the word.

I do miss the guys on the street and when I get a chance I go down and see them. But the supported housing and employment project was probably the best thing that ever happened to me. It literally changed my life. The sense of relief was incredible. I've never felt relief like it. It has given me my self-esteem and my self-confidence back and made me believe in myself again. Because when I was street homeless, I was at my lowest and I had no confidence, no self-esteem.

Heroin cost me a lot. It's cost me my children, my grandchildren. I've never even seen my grandchildren; the eldest is four. I've got a photo of her, but I've never seen her. It cost me everything, it wasn't worth it. I have so many regrets.

I've become really good at having rooms in my head with locked doors and if the thoughts do come out now I literally just shut the doors in my head and turn it off. I don't know how I do that, but I've become expert at it. If I go into town for an appointment and I walk past a doorway I slept in, I actually have to physically cross the road so I don't walk past it because I don't want to be back in that place. I'm thinking, 'I slept in that doorway, I slept in that bush, I cleaned my teeth in that public toilet.' It is always there, it is part of who you are, although it is a really unpleasant part of who you are. I think I am a pretty strong person and I survived it, but inside I am still just a child and I still need the reassurance. So by avoiding those doorways, that is me protecting myself. I don't want it thrown in my face and I don't want to be defined by the fact that I was homeless.

I think people should know homelessness can happen any time to anyone. It was one bad decision that cost me everything. It can happen to anyone. I think that is one thing that the public don't get, that it could be them. I would like people to accept that we are all different but we are all human and one bad decision doesn't define someone. It is what we do after that bad decision that defines them, so don't judge, is basically what I'd say.

Arna

WHOSE CITY IS IT ANYWAY?: THE CLEANING OUT OF CITY SPACES
ANNA MINTON

'Bubba, Big Black, Kizer and Red are the street names of four men who have said they served on squads that beat up the homeless.' So begins an article in *The New York Times* published more than twenty years ago, in 1995. 'They said that in recent years, while working for the Grand Central Partnership, they and others threatened, bullied and attacked homeless people to force them from doorways, bank vestibules, plazas and sidewalks all over Manhattan,' the piece continued.

It has long been a reliable rule of thumb that what happens in America tends to be repeated in Britain a decade or so later. And so it was with a whole raft of policies designed to make places 'clean and safe' and to 'reclaim the public realm' which have taken root in the US over the last generation. Keeping places clean and safe sounds like an appealing idea, because who, after all, would wish to live in a dirty and dangerous city? But an equally pertinent question is: who and what are we reclaiming the public realm from?

The answer was and is a wide range of infractions from homelessness, begging and busking to various activities generally associated with healthy and vibrant street life in the city. In the UK a toxic combination of policies lifted almost word for word from the US have redefined and reconfigured towns and cities, creating large areas where behaviours and activities are strictly controlled and access is conditional, open only to those who observe the rules. Chief among these overlapping policies are 'Secured by Design', the establishment of Business Improvement Districts (BIDs) and the privatisation of public space through the spread of privately owned streets and public spaces.

On the ground the result is the proliferation of defensible architecture, reaching its zenith in the anti-homelessness spikes designed to prohibit the homeless from sitting or lying on the pavement. Sloped surfaces, bench barriers and the practice known as 'wetting down'—which sees state-of-the-art cleaning equipment and power hoses used to literally clean out the homeless from spaces—are also part of this picture.

So how did we get here? In a society that lauds property ownership, homelessness is the ultimate affront. The paradox is that since the reification of property ownership became embedded during the 1980s, homelessness has also become a defining feature of British towns and cities in a way that it never was before. I remember being away from London for a few months in the late 1980s and coming back to see homeless people bedded down all along the Strand; prior to that I had never seen anyone homeless in London

ANNA MINTON

apart from the few who were part of the daily landscape. It was in this context that the government minister Sir George Young famously commented that the homeless are 'the people you step over when you come out of the opera'.

Although rough sleeping and large-scale homelessness didn't really exist before the 1980s, the defensible space policies which would be used against the homeless long preceded this and began in the early 1970s — again in the US. Oscar Newman, a Canadian architect researching crime in housing 'Projects' in New York, was a pivotal figure in this regard, although the fact that his work found such a ready audience on both sides of the Atlantic is undoubtedly because it chimed with the political mood of the time, anticipating the rise of neoliberalism. Newman's ideas amounted to no less than a new political and intellectual philosophy that expounded the virtues of private space, individual responsibility and territoriality. It began as a design philosophy aimed at housing, with the idea of preventing crime, but its application has now spread to include every facet of public space and public buildings, from streets, squares and civic spaces to schools and hospitals.

The context for Newman's seminal book *Defensible Space: People and Design in the Violent City*, published in 1972, emerged in a climate of concern over a rise in crime in urban America. He provided a relatively simple and cost-effective solution, arguing that rather than engaging with complex social problems as the causes of crime and disorder, design could offer 'can do' solutions that people could take responsibility for and which, he claimed, worked even in the poorest areas. From his study of three Projects he found that 'territoriality' created space that could defend itself, taking aim at the modernist design of tower blocks in particular (Manhattan skyscrapers notwithstanding). Clearly marked out boundaries would give residents a sense of ownership, discouraging strangers (and criminals) from entering.

Despite influential critics who condemned Newman's simplistic environmental determinism, his ideas spread like wildfire through American policy-making circles and substantial funding was made available for the implementation of his defensible space concepts which became known as CPTED — Crime Prevention Through Environmental Design. By the late 1980s the policy had made its way to Britain where it was called Secured by Design. Today, Secured by Design standards are a condition for planning permission on all new development in the UK and in particular for housing, schools, public buildings and public

WHOSE CITY IS IT ANYWAY?

spaces — an approach which is also boosted and justified by concerns over terror attacks. The ultimate 'private-public partnership', Secured by Design is a collaboration between the Association of Chief Police Officers and private security companies, with the Secured by Design website linking directly to four hundred security companies, which provide everything from prison fencing sold to schools to anti-ram bollards.

It is an approach which sits easily alongside the growing privatisation of public places, through a combination of private estates and the spread of Business Improvement District companies which run large parts of the city. The governing mantra of private places (known by their advocates by the acronym POPS, for Privately Owned Public Spaces) is the need to keep places 'clean and safe'. Digging beneath the appealing narrative, it emerged that this was a strategy instituted by the New York Mayor's office in the mid-1990s, which laid out guidelines for Business Improvement Districts to follow, according to the management structure laid out by management psychologist Abraham Maslow's Hierarchy of Needs. This famous pyramid structure, which is central to motivational psychology and has now been adopted by tens if not hundreds of thousands of management guides, created a diagram relating to what humans need to flourish. At the base of the pyramid is food, water, sleep and sex, followed by love and esteem and, at the top tier, peak experiences and 'self-actualisation'. As for the BIDs pyramid, that is geared towards creating the optimum trading environment and the first layer on which the whole structure depends is the creation of a 'clean and safe' environment, followed by transport and access, marketing and branding of the area and, at the top, the creation of a 'memorable experience for visitors'. When I was researching my book *Ground Control*, a manager of a BID company in Kingston described to me how the BID had carried out focus groups to find out what people wanted, and the answer came back that the number one priority was a 'clean and safe' environment. One can only assume incredible coincidence, or that the surveys were leading, to say the least.

In this new urban environment it can be difficult to tell who is in charge of parts of the city, blurring lines of accountability, as privately owned estates might employ BID companies to work for them. But equally BID companies manage large parts of the city where streets and public spaces still fall under local authority control. The upshot in every case is numerous uniformed officials: both cleaning staff operating state-of-the-art cleaning equipment and a range of security personnel, from rangers and wardens

ANNA MINTON

to ambassadors who act as security guards and are all working to the 'clean and safe' agenda. Unsurprisingly, keeping homeless people out of these areas, as *The New York Times* reported, was at the centre of the Grand Central Partnership BID's approach, and continues to be a key driver of BID activities in the UK. Although there are few reports of assault on homeless people here, a security manager working for a BID told me: 'We're not supposed to touch homeless people to wake them up because that's considered assault, but where I worked before, they do that, they're more "hands-on".'

Alongside the rise of BIDs the UK's towns and cities have witnessed the creeping privatisation of public space through the spread of privately owned estates, which abide by strict defensible space rules and are policed by private security according to the 'clean and safe' criteria. During the boom years which preceded the 2008 financial crisis, and which witnessed a wave of new construction across the UK, it became clear that privately owned estates, such as the financial districts at Canary Wharf and the Broadgate Centre, had become the template for all new develop-ment in the UK. While these two financial districts — built during the 1980s in the former industrial heartlands of East London — pioneered today's approach, this model, which was originally built in the image of business to serve the needs of finance, has come to define all new development.

To take just one example, Liverpool One, which was built just before the financial crash, is an enormous open-air mall which covers thirty-four streets in the heart of Liverpool, all of which are privately owned and policed by uniformed private security who enforce strict rules and regulations on behaviour and access. It is the same at Cabot Circus in Bristol, Westfield Stratford City in London and countless other 'malls without walls'. In addition to homelessness, begging, rollerblading, skateboarding, cycling and even eating and drinking in some areas, these places also ban photography, filming and, critically, political protest, which means that they are not democratic spaces. Ironically, even the headquarters of London's Mayor, the Greater London Authority, is part of a privately owned estate called 'More London', with the consequence that democratically elected Assembly members are prevented from conducting television interviews outside their own building.

Advocates claim that the Georgian squares and terraces which include some of the most beautiful parts of London were built on a similar model, by aristocratic landlords who controlled the 'great estates', such as the Duke of Westminster who owned

WHOSE CITY IS IT ANYWAY?

large parts of Mayfair and Belgravia and the Duke of Bedford who owned Covent Garden. What they don't say is that during the eighteenth and early nineteenth centuries, the great estates were closed to the general public, surrounded by high fences and railings and policed by security guards and sentry boxes, to ensure 'no tramps, vagrants, organ grinders, bands of musicians, or disreputable characters are permitted on the estate'.[1] As local government grew in power, paralleled by the increased democratic representation which came with the widening of the franchise, large-scale public protests took place against the gating off of such large parts of the city. By 1864–5, after two major parliamentary enquiries, 163 miles of road were passed over to local authority control and 140 toll bars were removed. Since then it has been customary for local authorities to 'adopt' streets and public spaces, to use the official terminology, meaning that whether or not they actually own them, they control and run them. This was a hard won democratic achievement which is now being reversed.

For the last decade at least, the consequence of the creeping privatisation of space in British towns and cities has been a game of cat and mouse between security personnel and the homeless, who are banned from certain parts of the city. Well over a decade ago, the 'tent cities' in the US, which clustered on the city peripheries, outside BID areas and private POPS, seemed to be setting a template for spatial segregation in British cities. But if the US has set the scene for where we might be headed, it seems an unprecedented crisis could be brewing. Rough sleeping in the UK has doubled since 2010 and it remains on the agenda for policymakers as the most visible sign of homelessness and the housing crisis. Today, little reported in the British media, American rough sleeping is turning into a humanitarian crisis across West Coast cities. In Los Angeles, even the BIDs can't keep out the homeless and in downtown areas tents line the streets three deep. For the UK, the only hope is that this trend isn't also the shape of things to come.

1 P. J. ATKINS, 'How the West End was Won: The Struggle to Remove Street Barriers in Victorian London', *Journal of Historical Geography*, XIX:3 (July 1993), pp. 265–77.

ANNA MINTON

← N

2
•
WHERE I SLEPT
LAST NIGHT:
Outside St Paul's Cathedral

BEKKI PERRIMAN

NTERVIEW
Emma

It all started when I was staying in my ex-partner's and experiencing domestic violence. It was getting to the stage where he was hitting me so badly I didn't know whether I was going to survive or not. I just woke up one morning and I couldn't take it anymore. I just walked. I had nothing; just the jacket I was wearing. I walked out, and he was like, 'Where are you going?' and I said, 'I'm going to the shop, I'll be back in a minute,' but I've not looked back since. It was frightening but the way it was getting, I was in fear for my life. To be honest, I know it is going to sound crazy, but I feel a lot safer sleeping on the streets.

I tried to get help. I went to this advice centre nearly every day and they kept on telling me the same thing: everywhere is full. They tell me to try Women's Aid, but Women's Aid tell me to try the advice centre and it's just going around in a circle. Then you go back the next day and there is still nothing and they tell you to try again tomorrow. It's been almost a year now and I am still sleeping rough, they still haven't found me anything.

The first night on the streets was the most scary, horrible feeling of my whole life. I meet people who say, 'How did you get through that first night?' I came into town and I was sitting there begging and I was like, 'What the hell am I doing?', and I was obviously trying to stay safe and stay away from my ex-partner. This woman called Susan asked, 'When did you become homeless?' and I told her it was my first night. She said, 'It's your first night on the street, you are a young girl, why don't you stick with us and get to know the routine.' If it wasn't for some of the girls, I don't think I would have survived it.

So, I hung out with the girls — Susan, Shoney and Melissa. We slept in an alleyway in one of the shop doorways and we got our sleeping bags and we just all huddled in together. We slept together for safety, because we get it constantly off men, dirty old men putting it nicely. 'What would you do for this?' 'Nothing.' 'But how about I give you twenty pounds if you do this to me?' What part of 'I don't want to' do they not understand?

One guy said to me yesterday, 'What would you do for me for eight pounds?' I said, 'I would tell you to leave me alone.' He was just so persistent it's unbelievable, it was horrible. One night, I woke up and there was this man standing in my doorway playing with himself. It's absolutely disgusting, it's horrible. Three, four, five, six times a day. It's always the same ones that keep on asking you. It's very downgrading.

It was the three girls, who were just amazing. Shoney, Melissa and I, we are all in our late twenties and Susan's older, so she just mummied us, she kind of looked after us and made sure we were alright. She was like, 'Have you had something to eat today?' and if you hadn't she'd get you something. They know what you are going through because they've been there, whereas I've got friends who've never been homeless, and you are trying to explain what it's like but they never understand. But with the girls we relate to each other.

I'm still in the same alleyway. I don't know where Susan is now. Shoney sleeps in another shop doorway and Melissa has got her own flat now. My doorway is tiny, it's absolutely tiny. I've got to sleep curled up, in a little ball, with my knees right up to my chest. There are two to three steps that go up to it, but it's just a wee, tiny doorway. I've got my dog with me now, but he just sleeps. He sleeps more than I do. Don't get me wrong, if there is someone passing, he kind of puts his head up but then if someone comes over, he just licks them. He is still a pup really. He's not at the stage of keeping everyone safe; he's at the stage of just wanting to play and lick everybody. He's not a guard dog at all, not unless you want to be licked to death.

In the winter we've got a night shelter and we go there from 10 o'clock at night until 7 o'clock in the morning and it's like a big massive room for women and another big massive room for men and it's just blow-up mattresses. It's from November to March, so that was alright, but it's trying to get there by 10 o'clock at night and then being kicked out at 7 o'clock in the morning. It'd be pelting rain up to your knees and you've got to get in the queue by 9 o'clock as there is only a limited number of beds, so you would never know if you would get in or not each night.

Being on the streets is boring, to be honest. You are just sitting there, bored out of your head and the way people look down on you is just horrible. One woman and her husband said to me

Emma

the other day, 'Have you got a job?' and I'm like, 'Oh my god is she being serious?' But it is very boring, very long and boring. If I've got a doctor's appointment or something now, I'm quite glad of it, just to go somewhere different instead of just looking at the same thing constantly and getting so many people walking past you, looking at you as if you are a piece of dirt on the floor. People assume that we are all drug users and alcoholics because you get that constantly, people telling you, 'Don't use that money on drugs,' and I tell them I don't use drugs and they say, 'Aye, of course you do.' Then it's, 'Don't use that money on alcohol.' I say I don't drink, and again they say, 'Aye, of course you do,' like they know me better than I know myself. People think that we are all drug addicts or alcoholics and, don't get me wrong, many people are, but they are trying to survive and trying to survive is the main thing.

It's so boring. Honestly, it's so boring. You've been sitting there, and you think it's five hours or something and then you look at the clock and it's only been half an hour. It's very boring. Friday and Saturday night are just horrible, it's so busy, with fire engines, ambulances, police cars constantly, it's so hard to get to sleep. It's hard to get to sleep any night, but on a Friday and Saturday night it's worse. You get people flicking fags on you and kicking you and then throwing stuff all over you. They think it is hilarious.

The way I got brought up by mum and dad was 'treat people the way you want to be treated' and the way some people treat you, it's just disgusting. Why would you want to walk along and put a cigarette out on someone's head?

I've got post-natal depression so I've got to take medication but sometimes it's really hard and I keep getting complaints off my doctor for not taking my medication properly. I try and explain to him that I'm homeless and sometimes I can't eat for days. When I became homeless my mental health went right downhill. When I'm having a bad day it's horrible, it is really horrible.

Some days you are just sitting there on your own, just doing nothing at all and you want anybody to come and talk to you. Just a bit of acknowledgement, because we are human, we have got feelings. Some days you just want for someone to come over and say hello and just to speak to you instead of always feeling so invisible. A few people have come over to me and said, 'I haven't got any money.' It doesn't matter whether you've got money or not, I'm only asking for a bit of conversation.

INTERVIEW

Yesterday someone said, 'I've not got any money but hello how are you?', and you are like, 'Thank god!', I don't care if you have got money or not, just please talk to me. Then there are other days I don't want anybody to talk to me and I'm like 'Just leave me alone,' and those are the days that everyone wants to talk to you.

Emma

SEEN AS UN-SEEN: HOMELESSNESS AND VISUAL CUTURE
MARY PATERSON

They are certainly more visible, aren't they? We've all seen them, more. More people begging on public transport, more people sleeping in doorways, more people sitting cross-legged with their heads bowed, their bodies still, their cardboard signs asking for pennies towards a night in a hostel.

According to official figures from the Department of Communities and Local Government (DCLG), the number of people sleeping rough in England has more than doubled in the seven years since 2010. They estimate over 4,000 people were sleeping rough in 2017, up 16 per cent on the previous year, and compared to 2,000 seven years ago.[1]

We've all seen them, more. Glimpsed their dirty fingernails in the moments before we flick our eyes away. Heard their raspy breath as we fumble to put our headphones in our ears. Almost tripped over their silhouettes as we scurry from the station, up the hill to home.

But the figures are unreliable — mostly an estimate based on a snapshot of rough sleepers guessed at by third parties and forwarded on to local authorities. In 2015, the UK Standards Authority publicly criticised the way this data is collected.[2] In contrast, the CHAIN (Combined Homelessness and Information Network) database counted more than 8,000 people sleeping rough in 2015–16, in London alone.[3]

The numbers are right about one thing, at least: homeless people are always seen and not seen, at the same time. 'People are not nice to me now,' says a homeless man interviewed by Megan Ravenhill for her book *The Culture of Homelessness*:

> Most people walk straight by, as if you're nothing, as if you don't exist. Some look down their noses at you. Some are really horrible and call you names. Kids are the worst because they come up and kick you when you're lying down. They can give you a right kicking.[4]

This kicking is real and symbolic. Ravenhill describes the culture shock that accompanies rooflessness. To be street homeless is to be rejected, profoundly, by mainstream culture. Once you're on the streets, you're simultaneously ignored, looked down upon and assaulted by people who are not. A 2016 report commissioned by the charity Crisis found that rough sleepers are fifteen times more likely to be abused than anyone else; more than half of perpetrators are complete strangers — members of the general (housed) public.[5] To be street homeless, then,

MARY PATERSON

is to be no longer visible as a member of mainstream society, but all too visible as something else: a punchbag, perhaps; or a cautionary tale.

We've all seen them, more. But we may not have really seen them. I once lived in a building with a good, wide door set back from the pavement. I stepped over a sleeping body most mornings. Curled like a cat. I never asked her name.

The culture shock that Ravenhill describes is a form of enforced withdrawal. It is the act of society being withdrawn, and it is not mutual. 'Instead,' she writes, 'society pushes [homeless people] out of the mainstream and isolates them.' Newly homeless people find themselves suddenly looked upon in a degrading and dehumanising way by many members of the public. It then becomes a matter of survival to acclimatise to living on the streets; people need to adapt and find a way to cope with the 'traumatic shock of sleeping rough'. Finding yourself in a situation of homelessness means learning how to survive — where to find food, sheltered places to sleep and a begging pitch (if needed). Newly homeless people are 'forced to learn how to look, act and speak like the roofless in order to survive both mentally and physically'.[6] Survival is a matter of being absorbed into homeless culture, which offers some comforts in the form of social networks, insider knowledge and physical protection. Survival means adopting the identity of a homeless person. But adopting the identity of a homeless person means giving up your identity in other ways.

They are certainly more visible, aren't they? We've all seen them: the posters. Grim looking scenes overlaid with large text instructing us not to give money to people begging in public places. 'Your kindness could kill', say the words, in bright yellow, on a poster designed for the homeless charities Thames Reach and Broadway London. 'Begging: watch your money go up in smoke', is the message from Nottingham City Council's 'Give Smart' campaign. The subjects of the posters are the people who have adopted the identity of a homeless person — who have learnt how to avert their eyes when they ask strangers for help; who have learnt where to stand and where not to sit in order to avoid, for as long as possible, the threat of violence.

The French philosopher Jacques Rancière describes politics as an activity, rather than a set of ideas. Politics is the activity of calling into question the 'distribution of the sensible' — the implicit ordering of the world: its rules and regulations, its memberships and permissions, its longings and desires.

SEEN AS UN-SEEN

The police or police order, in contrast, is the system by which the sensible is maintained. Order and politics, then, are always at odds. Politics will always disrupt order. And order will always fight back.

The subject of these posters is homeless people, and the audience is you and me. The campaigns share a clear, two-part call to order: 1. Don't give your money to people begging on the streets; 2. Give your money to the people who make the posters, instead. The point is to sever a direct connection between you and me (us), and homeless people (them), by suggesting one simple truth: we cannot believe what we see. When we see a homeless person begging for pennies, we cannot believe it's someone asking for help. Believe, instead, in a drug addict tricking us to fund her next fix. Believe in a liar imploring us to support her self-inflicted lifestyle. Believe in a person incapable of meeting her own needs, but nevertheless culpable for her own incapacity. In another poster, Nottingham Council makes both the blame and the conditions of visibility crystal clear: 'BEGGING', it shouts in capitals, over a picture of a man who meets your gaze: 'watch your money go to a fraud'.

Watch your money. In all of this, you and I are positioned as the people who watch. They—homeless people—are the ones who are seen. Seen but not believed. Seen, but not seeing back. (To look back, as Nottingham City Council knows, is a clear indicator that 'they' are up to no good.) A beggar worthy of contempt, a neighbour who'll never have a name; for people living on the streets, being seen and un-seen—being seen as un-seen— is a condition of existence and a deadly trap. We order the visibility of street homeless people, in order to insist that there is nobody (that is, nobody like us) there.

Democracy, Rancière continues, is a form of politics that reveals the existence of the *Demos* (the people) who are normally ignored or invisible in the distribution of the sensible. In The Doorways Project, the *Demos* made visible are the normally hidden and shunned members of homeless culture. In this context, the visibility does not hinge on homeless people being seen exactly, but on the potential to resist the ways in which homeless people are un-seen, day to day. They are un-unseen, perhaps, through an eruption of dissensus that threatens the order and exposes its networks of power. Here is a moment of democracy—or, more accurately, a democratic activity—that disrupts the order of (for example) the posters that tell us what to believe and what (not) to see. Likewise, the project disrupts

MARY PATERSON

the order of government agencies like the DCLG which, according to the UK Statistics Authority, observe homeless people and then manipulate the data for their own ends.[7]

The principles at stake here are not just to do with power, but also to do with money. As Matt Broomfield points out, there is a strange double-accounting that takes place when councils or homeless charities ask you to give money to them instead of to homeless people directly.[8] These agencies take credit (or direct debit, cash or cheque) for helping homeless people, while reinforcing the prejudice that maintains their exclusion from society. These agencies reinforce the oppressive conditions of visibility for homeless people, and profit from those conditions at the same time. Their posters are not public service announcements but adverts, using charitable and public funds to sell themselves as the seers and the saviours of the ones they mark un-seen. Watch your money, indeed.

But what of the order of homelessness itself? Ravenhill points out that for every 'push-factor' that drives people out of mainstream culture, there is a corresponding 'pull-factor' that draws them into the value system of life on the streets. She describes an inverted hierarchy, in which people who have survived the most are treated with respect, and not shame. The very same experiences that may have led to being rejected from mainstream society — childhood abuse, war, mental health problems, family breakdown, poverty, unemployment, or a complex combination of these and other issues — are reconfigured inside homeless culture as a kind of common ground: a way to start building relationships instead of being excluded from them. If you find yourself being or close to being roofless, induction into this alternate social system can be a vital means of psychic as well as material sustenance.

Ravenhill's analysis is a damning indictment of the society the rest of us live in. From this point of view, homelessness is not a problem but a survival strategy, developed in response to a brutal social order that kicks its most vulnerable members when they're down. In fact, the real problem lies in a culture that creates the conditions for homelessness and then polices its own borders to ensure those conditions are kept. This is less about behaviour than about the need for exclusion; less about resources than about access; less about 'them' than it is about 'us'. In the English language 'to see' is often synonymous with 'to know'. So it is no surprise that this problem resides in a type of hyper-visibility imposed on people who have always and already been rejected out of hand. By refusing to see homeless people as members

SEEN AS UN-SEEN

of our society, we also fail to comprehend homeless people as individuals, as survivors, or as agents in their own lives.

The principles at stake here are not just about power and money, but also competition. After all, we've all done it, haven't we? Walked past the body of another human being who shelters on our streets. Rushed home without opening our wallets for the silhouettes sleeping in the station. Felt the weapon of compassion rupture our progress, and screwed our minds shut until we couldn't feel the pain.

1 PATRICK BUTLER, 'Number of Rough Sleepers in England Rises for Sixth Successive Year', *The Guardian* (25 January 2017), available at www.theguardian.com.
2 UK STATISTICS AUTHORITY, 'Assessment of Compliance With the Code of Practice for Official Statistics: Statistics on Homelessness and Rough Sleeping in England', produced by the Department for Communities and Local Governments, Assessment Report 320 (December 2015), available at www.statisticsauthority.gov.uk.
3 BUTLER, 'Number of Rough Sleepers in England Rises for Sixth Successive Year'.
4 MEGAN RAVENHILL, *The Culture of Homelessness* (Aldershot: Ashgate, 2008), p. 157.
5 BEN SANDERS and FRANCESCA ALBANESE, '"It's No Life At All": Rough Sleepers' Experiences of Violence and Abuse on the Streets of England and Wales', report commissioned by Crisis (December 2016), available at www.crisis.org.uk.
6 RAVENHILL, *The Culture of Homelessness*, p. 158.
7 PETER WALKER, 'Statistics Watchdog Warns Government Over Homelessness Figures', *The Guardian* (22 February 2017), available at www.theguardian.com.
8 MATT BROOMFIELD, 'Why You Should Give Money Directly and Unconditionally to Homeless People', *New Statesman* (24 October 2017), available at www.newstatesman.com.

MARY PATERSON

← N

3
·
WHERE I SLEPT
LAST NIGHT:
South Bank

BEKKI PERRIMAN

INTERVIEW
Mwiinga

I have some experience of trying to get help from the council. I'll tell you one story. I was with my ex-partner for seven years. When we lived together, one evening there was a loud knocking on the door and when I opened the door someone just goes for me, someone punches me. Then they attacked my partner, kicking him, blood spurting all over the place, and they just left. They never stole anything. He was reluctant to go to the hospital because of the shock, but the next morning I took him there and he had broken ribs, teeth knocked out. When we got back, there was another knock at the door. Seven coppers were at my door and we were falsely accused of a crime, despite being victims of assault. We were in cells for twenty-four hours; that is the longest they can keep you in for. In that time, I never ate anything; I couldn't eat, and I couldn't sleep. I remember the police saying to me, 'What is your ethnicity, are you from around here?' They treated my partner completely differently. Because I am black, I got treated differently by the police. They put us in separate cells next to each other and we weren't even allowed to call a solicitor, but finally she was called. They dropped the case, because it was obvious we hadn't done anything wrong.

Within that time, we were moved by the housing association to a Travelodge for a week, but they wouldn't let us stay any longer than a week there because of cost. So, what do the stupid people at the housing association then do? They put us in a new place, 100 metres from where the incident happened. It's a derelict building. They have vigilantes there and they all know each other so I think they knew where we were. I couldn't sleep; there was banging, people pressing on the buzzer. My partner had gone out to the chemist for me and he had locked me in the house as we only had one key. I was feeling claustrophobic as people were banging on the door. I felt afraid, so I went out onto the balcony and I remember looking down and thinking, 'It's not too much of a drop, it's only two storeys, it's not that far.' I broke my ankle—my ankle was literally in reverse. My partner found me and so he called the ambulance and I spent about six weeks in hospital. I had to have three operations because my ankle was that damaged.

INTERVIEW

While I was in hospital I had to make sure I could sort things out for us. My consultant said usually in these places people get really depressed, but I tried my utmost to keep really strong. From my hospital bed I managed to get everything sorted out, housing benefit and ESA, because I couldn't work. Can you imagine trying to sort that out from a hospital bed? Eventually we were found a hotel and so we stayed there for two months. Then we went to another hotel which was a right shithole, did that for a couple of months and then they found us a studio. I remember looking at it and seeing how tiny it was and the state it was in and asking if we could have time to think about it, but they said no, and we had to make a decision there and then, so we took the place.

Things didn't pan out for us. I fell in love with another man, who became my fiancé. It was quite turbulent because we are both quite strong people and if you get two strong people sometimes it's not going to work because you have to have time and space. I was acting in a film. One day I got home after a day of filming and my fiancé was changing the locks. I asked him what was going on and he said, 'You are not welcome here,' and he had already pre-packed my bag. I tried to fight my way in. He said, 'But you called the police on me four times,' but I hadn't. The problem is when he got pissed he got aggressive and the neighbours obviously called the police and they arrested him. So, I just left.

I remember sitting on the kerb and it was getting late, so I thought, 'I need to get creative here.' So, I went to a bush. I saw this really secluded bush and so I slept there for the night and it was raining but I never got rained on. Another night after an argument I slept in a courtyard. No one saw me and luckily I had my bags on me with my scripts inside. It was a funny night because it was a hot day but that night it was very cold, and I had a jacket, but I felt the cold. I didn't really feel frightened. I don't know what was going through my mind. I felt angry with him, but I just thought, 'I've got no choice here. I've got to go to work in the morning. I have to focus, get my head down for the night and focus,' and that is exactly what I did. The next day at work I was fine, I stayed focused. Despite what troubles you have, you have to be professional, otherwise don't bother coming in. I thought, 'I've got to be positive.'

By kicking me out my fiancé put me a vulnerable position. I am very good at looking after myself and I'm lucky that I'm strong enough. All these bushes I've stayed in, they've kept me safe. There is one incident actually. There is this guy who comes to the garden and

Mwiinga

I was telling him about my situation and he said, 'You can stay with me.' So, I got to his flat and the first thing he told me was, 'I thought we were going to have sex,' and I just thought 'Oh god.' I felt really vulnerable at this stage and I got my stuff and I left. I slept in a bush. Safer than sleeping there.

As a woman on the street, you could get raped. My friend, she was on her way back from the bar and she got mugged, they took her mobile phone, they took everything. They see you as a vulnerable woman. I am strong, but I'm not strong enough if a man pounces on me, a woman alone in the dark, sleeping under a bush. At the garden for example, I got my bag stolen from there. All the crack-heads are coming in, people carrying knives, looking at people to rob — that's what it's all about these days and it's a shame really. It's not the way it used to be, so I try and avoid it these days.

The theatre company I work for, who knew about my situation, put me in a hotel for the night. I'd been there for the whole day trying to sort something out. We contacted the women's refuge, but they had no beds and so they decided to put me in a hotel and it was all paid for. However, when I got there, they said, 'Sorry you need a £50 deposit to stay, otherwise you can't have the room for the night,' and it was just because I was homeless that they did that. I tried to call work several times and I was embarrassed actually, because I thought they had organised it and I could just turn up at the hotel and get a bed for the night. In the end I called a friend and she put down the deposit, but if she hadn't have lent me it, I would have slept in a bush again. I felt embarrassed, really embarrassed. In a second hotel someone stole all my money off me, and then my mother arrived in the country and I don't want her to see me like this.

I made an appointment to see a housing officer at the council, but she was not very nice to me. They are very stern. She said you need your passport, which was difficult because it was at my ex-partners flat, but I got him to bring it into work for me and then went back. They photocopied my documents, but they haven't got back to me. She made me feel like I was nothing, like she was thinking 'not you again' or 'not another one again'. It made me feel really downgraded. It's bad enough that my fiancé threw me out, but as a housing officer she has a job to do, so why isn't she doing it? I find they are quite lazy and have no compassion. I don't know why they get jobs like that, because you have to have some kind of empathy, don't you. Why work in a homeless unit if you've got no compassion

INTERVIEW

and you don't genuinely want to help people? They've got no heart. I felt really downtrodden and like, 'here I go again'. I didn't even ask any questions, they just gave me a list of things to do and then I left.

'What now?', I was thinking to myself. It's the uncertainty because you don't know what is going to happen. 'Where am I going to stay the next night? Where am I going to be next month?' I am thinking, 'Shit, winter is coming and what am I going to do and where am I going to be?' That is what I was feeling. But I've got to put a lid on my feelings and stay focused, try and stay happy, whatever gets me through the day. The first week my fiancé threw me out I was in a state, which of course anybody would be. But every day I got a bit stronger and a little bit stronger. Baby steps and now I feel quite strong actually.

Kindness was a large element of what led me to homelessness; it's more effort to be horrible to someone than it is to be kind.

Mwiinga

POWER AND CONTROL: HOW THE HOUSING FIRST APPROACH CAN REDRESS THE BALANCE FOR WOMEN EXPERIENCING HOMELESSNESS

LISA RAFTERY

POWER AND CONTROL

Homelessness is often the result of the ultimate loss of power and control over a person's life. For women, in many cases, it is the result of domestic violence or other forms of abuse. Women become homeless to escape violence only to find themselves in a more vulnerable position once homeless. Research by Crisis and the Women's Rough Sleeper Project reported that women were more likely to experience sexual and physical assault while homeless than men. Violence and abuse remain common themes in women's experiences of homelessness.

Violence is about power and control: exerting power over another person and thereby taking away their self-determination and choice. One in four women will experience domestic abuse at some point in their lives, and for many women experiencing homelessness this will not be the first time they have experienced abuse. Adverse childhood experiences, such as child sexual abuse, physical abuse and neglect, are widely reported by women accessing homelessness services, and the traumas these result in are often pervasive. Recognising the role of power and control in the course of women's lives and how the loss of these intersects with homelessness is vital in the design of any services to support women. Many service approaches inadvertently re-traumatise women and replicate the power imbalance a woman has experienced throughout her life by taking away her choice and self-determination.

THE CURRENT LANDSCAPE

Since 2010 rough sleeping has increased by 169 per cent due to substantial changes to the welfare system, the impact of austerity, the national housing crisis and landlords ending shorthold tenancies. Alongside this, voluntary sector services supporting people who are homeless, women fleeing domestic abuse, mental health and drug and alcohol services have decreased due to large-scale funding cuts. These coinciding factors have contributed to the landscape within which women's homelessness is increasing, but with fewer services available to provide effective support.

Services that recognise women's multiple and intersecting needs are sorely lacking, and many women are either forced to sleep rough, sofa surf, exchange sex for a bed or access male-dominated services. In addition, when housing is finally

LISA RAFTERY

available, there is a lack of suitable options for women with multiple needs. The traditional refuge model is often not suitable, as many refuges are unable to accept women with high support needs, and with fewer refuge spaces overall, following large funding cuts to women's sector organisations, this presents a further barrier to women accessing women-only support. Women's Aid reported in their Nowhere to Turn report that 11 per cent of women slept rough and 40 per cent sofa surfed while waiting for a refuge space. A further 31 per cent of women with a mental health support need and 65 per cent of women with drug or alcohol support needs were refused a refuge space for this reason. In this context, it is important to acknowledge that mental health problems and drug and alcohol dependency often develop as a result of long-term experiences of trauma and abuse, rather than being a leading or contributing factor. What these women require is a gender- and trauma-informed service.

For many women who fall into this category the situation is dire; with no access to support or safety they often end up sleeping rough and turning to homelessness services which are not gender informed and are mainly male dominated, thereby placing women in positions of further vulnerability. Access to housing, once in this situation, can be a huge barrier to a woman's recovery from homelessness, trauma and abuse. Many services take a 'Treatment First' approach, requiring women to attend groups, engage with support workers, be assessed and reach certain goals before they are deemed 'ready' for housing. This, unfortunately, does not recognise women's priority for safety, choice and the need to regain control in order to rebuild and recover from multiple traumas. Women with multiple disadvantages do not experience addiction, mental health issues, homelessness and domestic violence as separate issues, but are nonetheless forced to access services separately and often without any coord-ination or communication between providers, which further hampers effective support. Holistic, coordinated gender- and trauma-informed services are vital in providing women with the range of support they need, through recognising women's intersecting disadvantages.

WHY HOUSING FIRST?

Housing First is exactly that: it provides housing first to women who may also be using drugs or alcohol as coping strategies, have mental health issues, have had contact with the criminal justice

POWER AND CONTROL

system or experienced the trauma of children being removed from their care. Women do not have to resolve these issues before housing is provided; instead, holistic, wrap-around support is tailored to the woman's needs, so that she can maintain her housing and recover from her traumas in a safe environment with access to support services which she controls. Housing First was first developed in the US in recognition of the fact that homelessness is often not simply a housing issue, but requires a coordinated response around the individual to support his or her recovery. There are now forty Housing First services in England following an evaluation of nine Housing First pilots in 2015. The key principles of Housing First focus on building control and choice, using a harm-reduction approach. Implemented well, the Housing First model has been shown to be an effective route out of homelessness for women.[1]

HOUSING FIRST FOR WOMEN IN PRACTICE

Threshold in Manchester provides a gender- and trauma-informed Housing First service for women experiencing homelessness with a history of offending. One of their peer support workers, who has lived experience of being supported by Housing First, encapsulated just how powerful this approach can be when delivered in a gender- and trauma-informed way:

> Women-specific services are making a difference to the lives of women … In my own experience, it's much easier to discuss issues like sex work, sexual violence or domestic abuse with a female worker or peer mentor. This is one of the only times that women begin to feel safe and have a sense of control over their own life … Women have a right to a care package that is sensitive to female presenting issues.
> – Linda, Peer Mentor

An evaluation of the first two years of the Threshold Housing First service by the University of York provides evidence for how and why this approach is working. In their interim report the researchers wrote:

> Women who have had multiple, hugely traumatic experiences over sustained periods of time, who have

run into difficulties and been let down by mainstream services, whose lives seem to have been characterised by both violence and an instability which for some must have seemed like chaos, have been successfully supported. There is evidence of strengthening self-esteem, improvements in health and well-being and growing ambition, moving way beyond the goals of older and more orthodox homelessness services.[2]

Women need to have power and control over their lives; sometimes what staff might think is a priority is not necessarily what a woman considers to be her priority, and simply asking what she needs is one of the most empowering things a service can do. Housing First, when delivered in a gender- and trauma-informed way, promotes choice and self-determination. A woman has the right to choose either to engage or not to engage in groups; to determine what support she needs and in what order she needs it; for her experiences as a woman to be recognised and understood; to feel safe in a home she is supported to maintain; and to recover in her own time knowing that the support is there to help her rebuild her life on her own terms.

POWER AND CONTROL

1 1 Everyone has the right to a home.
2 Flexible support is provided for as long
as it's needed.
3 Housing and support are separated.
4 Individuals have choice and control.
5 The service is based on people's
strengths, goals and aspirations.
6 An active engagement approach is used.
7 A harm reduction approach is used.

2 Deborah Quilgars and Nicholas Pleace,
'Evaluation of the Threshold Housing First
Project for Women Offenders: Interim Report',
Centre for Housing Policy, University of York
(November 2016), p. 36, available at https://hfe.
homeless.org.uk.

LISA RAFTERY

← N

4
·

WHERE I SLEPT
LAST NIGHT:
Hyde Park

BEKKI PERRIMAN

Susan

I wouldn't wish homelessness on anybody because sometimes you just feel like giving up. It's not a good thing; it's not good at all. A couple of times I felt like just ending it because of the way of life. It's a long day for somebody that is homeless because you've got to be out of the car park first thing in the morning and if it's not the attendant moving you, then it is the police moving you. So, you have to look for somewhere to go if you can't get back in at night. Some of the places I end up sleeping, I have no desire to be there at all.

I will disappear into a place where I can feel a certain amount of safety and I don't really tell anyone else where I am going. There is a young guy called Daniel who will come with me, because he actually feels safe with me and, likewise, I feel safe with him. Although I know, if it came to the crunch, I'd need to stick up for him. I'd need to be sticking up for the two of us.

There is a fair amount of abuse from people. I've been assaulted and had cigarette ash flicked on me. Someone threw flyers from a pub into the doorway when I was sleeping, and it clipped my eye and I couldn't see out of my left eye. They walk by calling me a tramp and all sorts of abuse. I've had a guy try to urinate on me, drinks thrown over me and all sorts of verbal abuse. It is like people are so ignorant, they just don't seem to grasp that we don't want to be homeless.

I sit in an area that is close to Daniel to watch his back and for him to watch my back. We sit close together when we are begging so we can look out for each other. I try and find a busy place with lots of people passing. That is not about money, that is about my safety. The more public the area I am sitting in the safer I feel.

This guy approached me last night, twice he approached me. I told him there is a difference between being homeless and prostitution and there is no red light above me. I felt quite intimidated because he kept coming back and I had to keep moving away. I am panicking inside, but I am pretty good at judging. I look right into somebody's eyes when they start to give me verbal abuse. I just shut up and

let every bit of verbal abuse go right over my head. No point arguing
with somebody like that because they are obviously looking for
an argument or a fight.

Being on the streets is tiring, draining. No two days are the same.
Every day is different. We were sleeping at the back of the car park
and a few people knew there were a group of us sleeping there. One
night we came back, and it's covered in piss and there were needles
all over the place. Why would people do that when they know
homeless people are sleeping there? You see blood splayed up the
walls — it is clearly not where you want to lie. You couldn't lie there,
anyway, because it's covered in piss.

There is a big drug problem on the streets, mainly smack, coke and
Valium, and if they are combined it is just fatal. There are quite a lot
of people who have overdosed this year. A guy who was homeless
for years, who I befriended, I don't know what he took but he never
woke up. He will be sadly missed. He always stood up for people
if they were getting hassle and he was really protective. I would say
the drug problem with homeless people is the fact that they are
homeless and there are a lot of people that I meet who have never
touched drugs before they are actually on the street. That's where
they meet up with other people and start getting into drugs and the
next thing you hear is that they have died, overdosed. It has been
a lot of people this year, but you never hear about it in the papers.
They don't care that another homeless person has died, they just
think, 'Oh, it's just another junkie.' They don't understand that
people end up dependent on drugs because of how crap their life
is, having to stay on the streets. I know it's not an excuse, but for
some people it helps the day go quicker. Sometimes you would
rather be sat with your head between your legs and pass the day
away than sit up straight because it is a very long day. It is too long
sometimes. Far too long.

I often sit by myself now just reading and ignoring people. That
is the only way I can cope, putting my head down into a book
and just ignoring everybody that goes by me. I feel invisible.

The winter is horrible because it is freezing. It doesn't matter where
you sit, you can't get warm. I spent the majority of the time camped
outside one doorway. There was a bank across the road which
is twenty-four hours and I could have been inside, where it is all
carpeted and indoors, but the police just move people on constantly

Susan

and you can't get away with sleeping in there. So, we just have to put on lots of extra clothing and all sorts of stuff. We would get two bins and polystyrene stuff and put that up to break the wind.

They were giving out extra sleeping bags to the homeless, because it was so cold, but you cannot leave anything because there is always somebody snooping about and the amount of thieving that goes on between homeless people is unbelievable. They would steal your shoes when you sleep. So, you don't really get your sleep as such. You are sleeping but it is not a deep sleep. You are just resting your eyes really because you don't know what is going to happen if you go into a deep sleep.

I think it is important for people to know that people don't go out of their way to make themselves homeless. There are a lot of people who understand, but clearly there are also a lot of people that are quite ignorant. If they really sat down and had a good think, who the hell would want to be sat outside in snow, rain, absolutely freezing conditions? Who would want to be sat out like that? Nobody. Nobody in their right mind. Yet, they go by you, being verbally abusive, and lob stuff at you like drinks and cigarette ends. People are not making themselves homeless intentionally.

I think there is a big difference being a woman on the street. I don't think the males get a lot of females going up to them and harassing them, whereas a female gets a lot of harassment and sexual innuendos. There are clearly some people that think that because you are homeless you are going to offer services to them and that is just ridiculous. They don't know your past, they don't know anything about you. In my past, I was sexually assaulted when I was eleven. So, people coming up to me and saying that actually does make me really intimidated by them.

That is why I like sitting amidst the other people. I feel safe. But at night when I want to go to sleep I need to be somewhere out of the way. A question that is always in the back of a female's mind on the streets: am I going to get sexually assaulted here?

In a hostel it is just as bad. You see, when you are down at a night shelter, you are watching your stuff because people are actually stealing other people's trainers and belongings. It is not right. It's places you clearly don't want to be in. There are people who are abusive to other people and they are abusive to the people that are working in these places. It is not good at all.

INTERVIEW

Being homeless my health definitely has deteriorated because it is not a normal life. It doesn't just attack your physical health, it attacks your mental health, because it does get really depressing. There are days that you feel like just giving up. You come out of the hospital straight out back to the streets and having to maintain taking medication every day — you can't — your life is sporadic. People would steal anything; if they thought that they could get a high off your medication, they will steal it.

When I went into the night shelter I had bags and bags, but you end up coming out with just one wee bag because people have stolen your stuff. You become dependent on the charity places to get clean denims, tops, jackets. You are depending on them for getting clean stuff. Last night I got absolutely soaked to the skin. It is no good for you when you are sitting with the same stuff on and it is not like you can take stuff off and hang it up and get it dried. If you are soaked it is hard to get changed and once those doors are shut at the night shelter then that is that. If there is any spaces, that is, and you can even get in at all.

It is definitely something that does affect your physical and mental health, being homeless. You meet some nice people, but you also meet a lot of horrible people and then there are the things that happen between that. It is one of the worst things that could ever happen to anybody — being made homeless. People don't have any idea what it's like being a homeless person, so don't go judging them.

Susan

STREET TALK: THERAPY OF PRESENCE
PIPPA HOCKTON

I founded Street Talk in 2005, when I was working as a therapi
in the NHS. I wanted to discover what psychological help, if
there was for women in street prostitution. I took a small ste_,
volunteering at a drop-in centre for women involved in street
prostitution in Hackney. I have worked with those women ever
since and their lives are so complex that I am still learning from
them thirteen years later.

The barriers to care for these women are many, and are
as complex as their own tangled life stories. There are a combination of psychological, emotional and practical issues which knit
together and make it virtually impossible for women in street
prostitution to get even the most basic help. There are practical
problems: a transient lifestyle, chaos, poverty, not having the bus
fare, violence, being beaten up, or being physically unable to get
themselves somewhere. Women's anticipation of prejudice, their
expectation — based on a lifetime of experience — that they will
be judged and humiliated by professionals, prevents them from
engaging with services. Being unable to access care, combined
catastrophically with these women's history of trauma, keeps
them trapped in a devastating cycle of exploitation, leading
to vulnerability and further abuse.

The systemic failures are too multiple to list here but
it is possible to outline those which are particularly destructive
in the lives of women living with trauma. Many of the women who
have come to Street Talk over the last twelve years have extremely
complex mental health histories, and it feels as though not enough
is known or understood to provide them with the care they need.
The women who come to Street Talk are catastrophically failed
by mental health services. Is it that women with complex needs
are too complex for mental health care providers?

The diagnosis of personality disorder seems to be used
as a blanket diagnosis, with little evidence of any treatment being
made available. It seems to be used as a label for patients who
exhibit challenging behaviour, closing down any further investi-
gation or professional responsibility. None of the women who
have had a diagnosis of personality disorder seem to have had
a thorough discussion with professionals about the meaning of their
diagnosis. Many only discover that they have been diagnosed with
a personality disorder when their medical records are investigated
as part of family proceedings. It is a diagnosis which serves
to dismiss them from mental health services, leaving them with
little understanding of their own mental health or hope of any
improvement in the frequently disabling symptoms which brought

about the diagnosis. I would go as far as saying that the words
'personality disorder' are less a diagnosis than a life sentence.

Women are refused access to mental health care, even
when they are in danger of self-harming or of taking their own
life. Looking back over thirteen years of case histories, not one
of the women Street Talk therapists have tried to have admitted
to hospital when they have been psychotic, or at acute risk of
overdosing, taking their own life or putting themselves in extreme
danger, has been admitted to hospital. Without exception, after
presenting at A&E at times of extreme vulnerability, the women
have been sent back out onto the street.

The most significant failure in mental health care for the
women Street Talk works with is an acute failure in the provision
of care for people with dual diagnosis. Approximately 70 per cent
of the street working women who come to Street Talk are dual
diagnosis. None of those women has ever been treated simultaneously for their addiction and their mental health issue. All of
them have been turned away, sometimes repeatedly, from mental
health services, on the basis that their mental health symptoms
are driven by their addiction. They were mostly signposted to
addiction services but were too mentally unwell to have the
capacity to engage, resulting in them being left with no access
to treatment. They were left on the street with neither mental
health care nor help with their addiction, with dire consequences,
including custodial sentences and even death. I am currently
working with a woman who was given a custodial sentence for
missing court. At the time, in the grip of a psychosis, she had
no idea what day it was or who she was, and was found by hostel
staff crawling naked in her room.

Among those responsible for the provision of care, there
is an ethos of personal responsibility which absolves welfare
services but blames the most vulnerable for their suffering. There
was an outpouring of public revulsion at the brutal abuse of Peter
Connelly in 2007. He was a baby and he wasn't held responsible
for what became of him; but how much public interest is there in
his siblings, who also lived through abuse and have had the usual
disrupted journey through the state care system? At what point
does sympathy fall away for a person who has had that kind
of start in life, and at what point do they begin to be held
accountable for their suffering? Almost all the women Street Talk
works with have lived through some version of the start in life
which Peter Connelly had, and although they have survived, they
have suffered unimaginable trauma. At some point along the way,

they find themselves held responsible and blamed for behaviours which are driven by the trauma they have survived. Since founding Street Talk I have been constantly frustrated by the widely held assumption that all women in street prostitution are here by choice. There are different kinds of prostitution which women choose to make a living from, broadly referred to as 'indoor prostitution', but nobody chooses street prostitution, where rape and violence are daily occurrences. To attribute street prostitution to choice is to collude with the abuse and exploitation which has brought a woman to that place.

It seems that the reality of the lives of women who have been repeatedly traumatised is unbearable for professionals to confront, resulting in a systemic, unconscious denial. This work has taught those of us working for Street Talk the meaning of the word 'unspeakable'. There are things that have happened, and which still happen to women, which are hard to speak about and which can't be written about here. It takes women years to tell some of what they have lived through and when you hear it you can't repeat it. This leads one to question whether one of the reasons professionals disbelieve women and deny their truth, is that this represents an unconscious defence from an unbearable reality. It may be that to deny the reality of these women denies one's own vulnerability. If a woman has become extremely vulnerable through no fault of her own, then, by extension, that can happen to anybody, which makes the world appear precarious and unsafe. If it should be the case that to acknowledge that the brutality the women have lived through is unbearable, is unconsciously pushed away, then how can professionals provide for their needs? There seems to be a vicious circle where denial of the reality of women's experiences prevents services from responding to their needs, keeping them trapped in a lifelong cycle of abuse and trauma. How many women and girls were subjected to prolonged abuse or even punished in Rotherham and how many professionals apart from the brave youth worker Jayne Senior chose to deny their reality? The women who come to Street Talk have experienced a lifetime of their reality being denied. No wonder they are reluctant to work with professionals.

The removal of children and the unseen grief which that brings is an overwhelming issue in the lives of many of the women who come to Street Talk. The poor care for vulnerable women with complex needs who become pregnant creates a further generation of vulnerability. Sometimes the process of child protection proceedings compounds a woman's sense of worthlessness. When it is necessary to remove a child from the care of a mother, it must be possible to do that with compassion, with humanity, to acknowledge the woman's trauma and to offer an appropriate intervention. I was present with a woman when social services came to the hostel where she lived, to remove her child. Two social workers arrived, with police, who rattled handcuffs at her, shouted at her to stand on the other side of the room, refused her permission to kiss the child goodbye and refused to accept the little teddy bear which she had knitted for the baby and wanted him to have. At the most vulnerable moment of her life, she was treated like a criminal. Suffering engenders further suffering. A woman who has her child removed as a result of her complex needs is unlikely to have the resources to recover from that experience on her own. Few women would. It is the responsibility of providers of mental health care to address that need, and it is not a need which is currently met.

Another systemic failure adding to the suffering of women in recent years has been the sanctioning of benefits. We currently work with a number of women who are street homeless as a result of interruption to their housing benefits, through no fault of their own, and although it has finally been proven that it was error on the part of the benefits agency, the harm has already been done. One of the women who was evicted from her home when her benefits were sanctioned was badly beaten up when she was on the street and suffered brain damage. After a year, her benefits were reinstated and paid back, but there is no reversing the brain damage.

Sometimes there is no evident solution to a homeless woman's problem. The challenge in those cases is to recognise that and not to try to invent a solution because it is too painful to acknowledge that there isn't one. There is a societal myth that if you work hard, roughly behave yourself, observe the law and exhibit good citizenship, you will be ok. There is an expectation that if the homeless get off the street, get a roof over their head, get off benefits and into work, start paying their own rent and contribute fiscally, their own problems will be solved and they will cease to be a problem to the public. It is not that simple; trauma is complex and it can take years to recover.

The women who have come to Street Talk have shown us how to adapt the service to respond to their needs. They have taught us the importance of accompaniment, of bearing witness. They have shown us how to make small, practical adaptations to the provision of therapy so that, for example, the therapy takes

place in hostels and day centres where the women feel safe. Base
on the women's choice, the service remains women only, to ens
that it is safe for the women to use, without being under the eye o
their exploiters, who for the most part are male. Most importantly,
women are not penalised for failing to attend or for arriving late
for appointments. Regular, weekly, fifty-minute sessions work for
people with organised lives.The women we work with live chaotic
lives as a result of their historic and current trauma, and so we
wait for the time when a woman is able to attend, however long
that takes. In some cases the wait has been years.

I have named the clinical model which has evolved over
thirteen years of work 'Therapy of Presence'. The name recognises
the importance of the therapist's presence, holding the space for
the woman, even at those times when she is not able to be present
herself. The aim of the work is to enable the women to encounter
their own humanity in the relationship with the therapist. The
women discover a relationship where the other person does not
want a piece of them, does not judge them, does not want to hurt
them. We are interested in what are referred to as 'soft outcomes':
women feeling self-worth, feeling human, getting some sense
of their own identity. The hard outcomes — exiting prostitution,
abstinence, getting out of exploitative relationships and so forth —
are important, but it seems that when the soft outcomes fall into
place, the hard outcomes follow. The value of the work is in the
human contact, irrespective of the outcomes which may ensue.
One woman told us after some years that her turning point came
when the Street Talk therapist passed her in the street, noticed
that her shoelaces were undone and bent down to tie them for her
because she had mobility difficulties and couldn't reach. She said
afterwards that in that moment she felt human again.

From the first woman who came to Street Talk at the day
centre in Hackney, to the one I worked with this morning before
sitting down to write this essay, we continue to learn from the
women what their needs are and how to shape our service to meet
those needs. The women know what they need, if only those
providing care would listen.

← N

5
•
WHERE I SLEPT
LAST NIGHT:
Outside Centre Point

BEKKI PERRIMAN

INTERVIEW
Tracy

I had a son in 1990 and in the nineties there was not really a lot of information out there about post-natal depression and I didn't realise I was suffering from it. I went away for a weekend as I was finding it hard to cope. While I was away, I met someone who was a drug dealer and I was staying with him. He gave me something on a foil, which I didn't realise at the time was heroin. We were smoking it every day. Then one morning we got raided, he was arrested, and I was on my own.

I couldn't even tell you the first night I slept rough although I can remember certain nights. I was sleeping rough for eighteen years and I was eighteen years on crack cocaine and a heroin addict. It started from smoking it, to then on what we call a pipe, and then I started injecting and it got so bad that I couldn't find a vein. I was skin popping which is just pushing the needle into fat or muscle, which caused me to be very ill. I've got loads of abscess scars. I'm just really lucky that I didn't lose any limbs because I was in a right state. Eighteen years just flew past. By the time someone had come to help me, I was like, 'Where did the years go?', because that was how bad my addiction was. I didn't know at the time I was struggling with a mental health issue. The streets became my way of life; it just became the norm for me. Getting up, taking drugs, getting money, going to the drug dealer, coming back—that was the cycle.

Being on the streets as a young woman, as a sex worker and homeless, there were many situations that were so traumatic. One night I remember getting raped twice and then still having to go back out there and lie down with a stranger just because I was trying to tend to my habit. A normal person wouldn't do that, they would go to the police, they would go to hospital, but an addict doesn't do that.

The days that I always remember were Christmas Days as that is the most lonely time, seeing everyone out with their relatives, seeing the children playing and all you are doing is sitting under a bridge. All you've got to look at is your dirty needles and your drugs. Christmas really stuck out for me—I felt so lonely. One Christmas I went on the high street looking for a customer, just so I could feel like I was a person. I remember selling myself to that man for £20 and that was just part of being included so I could be with someone and part of their Christmas. It was such a lonely time and I had the guilt of leaving my son. I'd be thinking about him and wondering what he looked like, wondering if he was ok. Being on drugs, I just pushed it to the back of my brain.

I gave my daughter up when I was on drugs. She was taken off of me and the thing was she wasn't taken off me because I was a drug addict, she was taken off me because I was homeless. There were no mother and baby units at the time. They had her adopted without my consent. I phoned up my mum; it was the first contact I'd had with my mum since being on the street. I left her a voice message, I said, 'Mum I've had a baby, her name is M, they have taken her from me, I don't know what to do.' The next minute I just lost it, security escorted me out, told me if I came back I would get arrested. So yes, I took the easy way out, I went and used drugs because it was the only way I could cope with it and I knew they wouldn't give her back to me, so I didn't fight for her.

I didn't know this at the time, but luckily though my mum did fight for her, my mum apparently turned up at the hospital the next day and they fought through the courts for visiting rights. When I finally did get in contact with my mum, when I came off drugs, eighteen years after leaving home, the first thing I said to my mum was, 'Did you meet my daughter?', and my mum said, 'Yes of course, we know her, she has met your son.' It wasn't the happy ending I wanted. I have to admit I own a lot of the guilt — she has feelings of rejection, she can't understand why I would have a child being on drugs. I wasn't having regular periods, I was on heroin, I was a sex worker, I was with a violent partner — my mind wasn't in the right place. If I could go back now there is no way I would have had a child, but I didn't know I was pregnant. It was only when I started having labour pains I realised, I knew I'd had those pains before. At that time, when I had my daughter, I couldn't do anything about the situation I was in, I was too in it and I'll feel guilty about that for the rest of my life.

The turning point was when I saw my outreach worker Mark who had spent the last year trying to convince me to get off the street and I'd always said to him 'No'. But this time I asked him, 'So what about this hostel you keep promising me then? Lets go.' Mark was totally taken aback because he'd been trying to work with

Tracy

me for a year. He made some calls but there weren't any hostels with beds available. He refused to give up and got me into a B&B and booked me an appointment for the following morning at the drugs advisory service.

Mark got me into a hostel. For me personally I don't think someone coming off drugs should be put in a hostel. You have to be so strong. Because you see it and you smell it and people are doing it in front of you. When my mum died I relapsed really badly but now I've not had a relapse for two-and-a-half years. So, I'm finally on the road to recovery. However, I would never class myself as safe. I would always class myself as in recovery.

If I was asked before I became an addict whether heroin was a personal choice or a disease I would have said it was a personal choice. But no; I believe it is a disease. There is still something in you that is niggling to get back up, whether it surfaces or not. People don't understand, they think it's a personal choice, but it's not. Once heroin gets hold of you, it doesn't matter what drugs the doctors give you, once that disease has got you, it will take your life if it can. I'm really lucky it didn't take my life. It took many of my friend's lives and that's a real shame.

I think there isn't enough support for women on the street. A lot of women struggle with mental health and there is a lot of stigma still out there. People also need to realise there are a lot more women sleeping rough than the statistics say there are, but women on the street are more hidden. There are so many women who are sex working and the rapes they go through, the attacks, the addiction, it's awful. There are lots of women with severe mental health problems. They end up in hospital, given heavy doses of anti-psychotics, and then are discharged straight back out onto the streets again. There is so much behind it and I don't think we have the resources.

The system needs to start retracing its steps and looking at it in a different way because it's still not changed from years ago. It's about sitting down, talking to the person, getting to the problem, and they may not open up in the first week, or the next few months, but it doesn't matter how long it takes, there is a reason why that person is struggling with these issues.

When I was picked up and put into a hostel, Mark my outreach worker knew that I was very vulnerable. It was really scary. I was on my own, he was my only contact. At the time I didn't realise I was struggling with depression and I think when you come off the streets and you are also coming off drugs, only then does it all hit you, all the emotions. It is too much for your brain to take. I think lots of people get lost then because of the severity of mental health, especially if they are on their own. I was lucky I had such brilliant workers 24/7 and knowing I had that support kept me going.

It's especially hard for women on the streets because you go into a day centre and there are always men there and if you are a sex worker, or you are a very shy girl, you are going to feel intimidated. To get to the root of the problem you've got to have a place where women can come for support where it is not all male dominated. Women walk into a lot of day centres and think, 'I don't feel safe here,' so they are not going to come back. All the places I know that are for women only are either religious led or its for a specialist area like drugs or sex workers, but there aren't many services that are safe spaces just for all women, whether or not they fit into those categories.

What people have got to realise is that we didn't want to come here and be homeless; something happened to us and it put us in that position. I never thought I'd end up being a drug addict or a sex worker—of course I didn't—but something happened to put me in that position, it became my way of life. I would like all the people who hurt me to look at me now and see that I got myself through this, they didn't define me with what they did to me. I got myself through with the help of support workers who took their time to help me and support me, who actually listened to me and who went that extra mile to help. I'm blessed, I'm really grateful.

Tracy

VIOLENCE AND TRAUMA: A SOCIETAL REALITY WE ARE ALL RESPONSIBLE FOR
LAURA E. FISCHER

Complex histories of abuse and neglect, particularly in childhood, leave an array of marks on the mind, the brain and the body. Trauma never comes alone, yet its many consequences are often the focus of the clinical eye, which assesses the presenting problems in isolation. Survivors of violence are frequently labelled with a series of separate diagnoses, while the core of the matter — the link between that which may present in a variety of forms, be it behavioural problems, substance dependence, suicidal ideation, or any of the many possible expressions, including physical conditions such as auto-immune diseases — is dismissed. I wish in this text to address some of the issues around the aftermath of violence; doing so through the lens of trauma permits a better understanding of the complexities of homelessness, not only because life on the streets is a weave of repetitive trauma but also because it is often traumatic experiences that force individuals to find themselves without the safety of a home, and the othering and stigmatisation that homeless people face highlights the severely damaging biases that society upholds.

We still foster naïve narratives of abusers as dark characters who come out to prey and victims as fragile innocents who cannot protect themselves from the big, bad, outside world. This dichotomy negates all of the nuances in between and, truly, almost all forms of violence occur in this in-between. Assailants tend to be much more akin to those they hurt and often the two entertain a form of relationship; in fact, it is commonly their interpersonal connection that is exploited by the abuser. Yet we continue to concentrate our questions — if not our accusations — on the victim's decisions and behaviours. Without shifting the focus of our interrogation on to those who violate instead of those who are violated, we will never attain an understanding of what makes abusers feel entitled to abuse, nor will we achieve a comprehension of the necessary actions we must take for this to change. I would argue further that our gaze must go beyond that of the individual's history and look at the socio-cultural environment. What I denounce is the societal context that permits these expressions of violence and abuse to occur.

I can still feel the burning pressure of the leather belt around my neck and the shiver down my spine as my cold bare feet were about to step off the chair. When I found myself in a hospital bed a doctor came to see me; she was the first psychiatrist I had ever met. I had attempted to end my life moments after seeing a photograph on social media of one of the men who had raped me, yet I did not recognise the link. I did not tell her about

LAURA E. FISCHER

the assaults, nor about the nightmares, the flashbacks or the blood I so often vomited. I said I was ok, but I was scared. I was afraid of what was happening to me. I was not able to understand, but that morning I was ready to accept: something was seriously wrong and I had to fight to survive. I promised myself I would do whatever it took to get better. That decision and the journey it led to were the most difficult steps of all. It is far harder to accept to heal than it is to accept to suffer.

It took months of drifting in and out of hospital before I could bring myself to concede that I had been at the receiving end of severe violence and that what I was battling with was trauma. Determined to comprehend this extensive denial, the mechanisms of traumatic stress and the socio-cultural context that allows these conditions to prevail, I decided to shift my practice towards psychology, psychiatry and neuroscience, and I have been working both independently and with the National Institute for Health Research (NIHR) Collaboration for Leadership in Applied Health Research and Care (CLAHRC) on opening dialogues about the consequences of violence and the silence we maintain around it, and on improving current trauma treatments by widening our understanding and approach. I have found that beyond the individual challenge of the neurobiological impasse a survivor faces when met with trauma, there is a vast societal problem that makes the communication of traumatic experiences almost impossible, and consequently the recovery extremely difficult.

This problem appears as an intricate and interconnected web of prejudice, a displacement of power dynamics, an estrangement of strength and vulnerability in our narratives, and an implicitly agreed universal silence. My story, like that of so many others, bears witness to our failure as a society. I had been raped, kidnapped and raped again repeatedly by a man who wished that I would be his. The first person I told about this did not believe me. He not only blamed it on me but he, too, raped me. When I screamed in agony as he touched me, he realised I had told the truth about my assault, but this did not stop him. On the contrary, he declared that it was his way of proving his love to me and that by this action I owed it to him to be his. With no evidence or reassurance that I could speak out about these abuses, I fled and told no one. This experience of sexual violence and male entitlement is not unique in any way; it is the chronicle of millions of women, irrespective of geography or ethnicity. Our society normalises the abuse of power and maintaining silence on issues that seem too hard to abide allows such dynamics of violence and abuse to prevail.

VIOLENCE AND TRAUMA

I believe our separation and distance when it comes to dealing with traumatic experiences is not a result of these experiences being foreign or uncommon, but is in fact because they are so widespread, pervasive and debilitating. Violence is omnipresent in today's societal climate; more than half of the population is exposed to at least one potentially traumatic incident in their lifetime,[1] and over a third of women experience sexual abuse, physical abuse, or both, at some point during their life:[2] trauma is not rare and it is not extraneous. It is right here, right now, and we are all implicated, directly or indirectly. It is the product of social, cultural, biological and economic factors and it has a societal cost that runs in the billions of pounds. It has been described as a hidden epidemic and named the most pressing unaddressed public health threat today, yet the culture we cultivate strips us from the resources we need to prevent and respond to trauma. We dichotomise narratives of (false) strength and victim-isation and we settle on a collective consensus to both distance ourselves from matters that concern us all and to demean survivors as victims defined by the abuse they were put through, often even blamed for what they endured.

We either invalidate a person's experience or classify them as a victim, reducing them to the passive receiver of violence. Neither of these narratives allow for individuals to be owners of their account, experts of their experience, or potential leaders of change. We are told as individuals, and tell others in turn, to be strong and move on, to be positive, but we are not fully aware of the implications these words may have. I believe that this approach not only indicates a common misconception but furthermore illustrates the contradiction that lies at the core of our culture. It is far stronger to acknowledge an issue, accept it and attempt to restore it than it is to bear the pain, dismiss what it calls for and carry on. Moving on in this way is not being strong or positive; it is being in denial. Being positive is not plastering a smile over a hard experience; being positive is recognising this experience for its negative nature and acting upon it to make it transformative. Acknowledgement allows for what denial forbids: a continuously evolving learning curve. Not moving on, but moving forward. Instead, our culture's momentum tends to be circular—and that pattern needs to be redirected.

Individuals who suffer from the trauma of extreme violence face a risk of suicide far higher than those without traumatic experience. According to the US Department of Veterans Affairs, approximately thirteen ex-soldiers commit

LAURA E. FISCHER

suicide per day in the US alone as a result of trauma. Not only is this a conservative estimate, but it is one of few statistics obtainable on post-traumatic stress, and most of these, as well as the majority of readily available information on trauma, are based on war veterans. Yet combat is not the main cause of trauma—abuse is. It appears as though the world can accept that a soldier coming back from a foreign war might be traumatised; but when the war is at home, in the form of emotional or sexual abuse, for example, the trauma is not validated. This is just one of the biases of public knowledge that, fuelled by economic interests, not only devalues a great quantity of experiences of violence but also precludes many survivors from accessing help. Trauma does not just wear an army uniform; in most cases, it is in ordinary clothing. And this should be the case for a significant share of the stakeholders involved in trauma responses, whether in research, interventions, treatments or policy-making. The people at the core of the matter must be at the core of the decisions that concern them.

Traumatic experiences vary in the type of violence inflicted, the source of the adversity, the duration and chronicity, the context, the different developmental stages and in the resulting imprints and the corresponding trauma diagnosis. They differ from other difficult experiences by the magnitude, intensity and abruptness of the emotional, mental and physical shock induced by the violence. This shock is the trauma: it expresses the loss of inter- and intra-relational safety and persists long after the traumatic events occurred, severely disrupting the individual's life. However horrendous the traumatic events, it is the trauma that is the most devastating: the body's natural stress response to threat fails to protect due to the extreme or pervasive nature of the adversity and is then prevented from rebalancing, effectively entrapping the traumatised individual in an altered state of dysregulated arousal. This has a direct impact on the brain's ability to record the information; due to arousal dysfunction, it cannot process the traumatic material as it normally does, encoding it as present body sensations as opposed to an articulated memory of the past integrated within the person's timeline. This essentially means that traumatised individuals live in a constant reality of violence. Experiencing inescapable intolerable sensations of the past, the lives of traumatised people therefore often become organised around neutralising these unwanted sensory experiences; making use, for example, of excessive alcohol or drug consumption, recurring self-harm or high-risk behaviours.

VIOLENCE AND TRAUMA

For adults, trauma is a truly distressing experience which can have lasting effects. For children and young people, however, the extent of trauma's impact is particularly severe, as the psychological, cognitive, social and biological development of children subjected to interpersonal adversity is pervasively modified. Biological correlates are in fact not only numerous but neurobiological alterations have been found to be more specific to childhood abuse than any other psychopathology. Trauma shapes the development of survivors' brains and bodies, altering their nervous system, immune system, hormonal system and even DNA, causing an array of mental and physical health issues, influencing self-destructive behaviours and impeding self-regulation capacities. This, all together, guides traumatised individuals' problematic relationships with themselves and with others, and impacts their life expectancy. In a longitudinal study conducted by Sroufe and Collins in 2009, aimed at understanding the developmental role of nature versus nurture and personality versus environment, childhood abuse and neglect emerged as the most important predictors of adult (dys)functioning and (ill) health.[3] To confront the reality of childhood trauma is to directly face the heart of the impact of the societal problem discussed here.

It is important to understand that this is not a minor issue either; millions of children's development occurs in dysfunctional caregiving systems with prolonged threat and exposure to maltreatment, abuse or neglect.[4] From a database of thirty-eight reports covering ninety-six countries, it is estimated that in a single year over half of all children aged two to seventeen years—that is one billion children globally—are subjected to emotional, physical or sexual abuse.[5] UNICEF furthermore affirms that such violence is vastly concealed and under-reported.[6] Meta-analyses of global prevalence of abuse suggest that child physical abuse is seventy-five times higher and child sexual abuse thirty times higher than official numbers.[7] Moreover, traumatised women with a history of childhood sexual abuse are twice as likely to experience harassment or assault than non-traumatised women,[8] whose risk is already high.[9] Overall, the direct and long-term repercussions of child abuse on public health, paired with the associated financial costs, decelerate social and economic growth, destabilise investments in health and education and corrode the productive potential of following generations.[10] It is estimated that eliminating child abuse would lower 'the overall rate of depression by more than half, alcoholism by two-thirds, and suicide, IV drug use, and domestic violence by three-quarters'.[11]

LAURA E. FISCHER

These are the reasons why the adults these traumatised children grow into are often the very ones we find in our detention centres or on our streets; not because they chose to be helpless, but because of the consequences of the violence imposed upon them, coupled with societal prejudice and a lack of accessible resources. We incarcerate people and take their freedom away, disregarding the fact that it was often the lack of this very freedom in a context of abuse and/or neglect that drove them to the benches of the court in the first place. We must question how many crimes and shattered lives might be prevented if we focused our efforts on optimising the circumstances in which children develop, as opposed to the repercussions of the lack of secure attachment, by which time the harm has already been done. Similarly, we are quick to blame homeless people for alcohol or drug addiction; instead of recognising what they signify and responding with appropriate support, their survival methods and coping mechanisms for either the traumas that led them to the streets or the trauma of being on the streets itself are deemed outside of societal norms, shamed and criminalised.

Stripped of the ability to fit into society's narrow story-line, these individuals see themselves facing an extreme form of othering and stigmatisation. Not only have they had to withstand the wits of injustice, but they are exposed to further violence because of it. The very people who embody the consequences of the problems we feed into, and who we should be focusing on readdressing, are the ones whose existences we erase and whose voices we mute. I would like to suggest a radical shift in this paradigm and a crucial widening of our perspective. I believe that resilience should be favoured over strength—that is, embracing vulnerability as an asset for growth—and I believe for this reason that these voices are precisely the ones that we should listen to and even allow to lead our steps towards positive change. And, critically, I believe that we must join our own voices to the conversation. We are not exempt. There are wider agendas that shape a singular story; violence and trauma are part of a dynamic that goes beyond the duality of perpetrator and victim. I don't believe it is a matter of the one or the other, or solely of one gender, one race, or one religion. I believe we are all contributors to a society that allows violence to prevail and I believe it is for us all to question how our individual actions might feed into this culture.

VIOLENCE AND TRAUMA

1 R. C. KESSLER et al., 'Posttraumatic Stress Disorder in the National Comorbidity Survey', *Archives of General Psychiatry*, 52:12 (1995), pp. 1048–60.

2 A. K. AGNIHOTRI et al., 'Domestic Violence Against Women — An International Concern', *Torture*, 16:1 (2006), pp. 30–40.

3 L. A. SROUFE and W. A. COLLINS, *The Development of the Person: The Minnesota Study of Risk and Adaptation from Birth to Adulthood* (New York: Guildford Press, 2009).

4 World Health Organization, 'Child Maltreatment', fact sheet (30 September 2016), available at www.who.int/mediacentre/factsheets/fs150/en/.

5 S. HILLIS et al., 'Global Prevalence of Past-year Violence Against Children: A Systematic Review and Minimum Estimates', *Pediatrics*, 137:3 (2016).

6 UNICEF, *Hidden in Plain Sight: A Statistical Analysis of Violence Against Children* (New York: UNICEF, 2014).

7 M. A. STOLTENBORGH et al., 'Cultural-geographical Differences in the Occurrence of Child Physical Abuse? A Meta-analysis of Prevalence Around the World', *International Journal of Psychology*, 48:2 (2013), pp. 81–94; M. A. STOLTENBORGH et al., 'A Global Perspective on Child Sexual Abuse: Meta-analysis of Prevalence Around the World', *Child Maltreatment*, 16:2 (2011), pp. 79–101.

8 J. HERMAN, *Trauma and Recovery: The Aftermath of Violence — From Domestic Abuse to Political Terror*, 2nd edn (New York: Basic Books, 2015).

9 AGNIHOTRI et al., 'Domestic Violence Against Women'.

10 World Health Organization, *INSPIRE: Seven Strategies for Ending Violence Against Children* (Geneva: World Health Organization, 2016).

11 B. VAN DER KOLK, *The Body Keeps the Score: Mind, Brain, and Body in the Transformation of Trauma*, 3rd edn (London: Penguin Books, 2015).

LAURA E. FISCHER

← N

6
·
WHERE I SLEPT
LAST NIGHT:
St Martin-in-the-Fields

BEKKI PERRIMAN

INTERVIEW
Jessica

I left home when I was nearly sixteen and I moved into a hostel which was for young people, mostly leaving care. It was a really difficult place to live and there was a lot of violence. One night a girl called Claire threatened us all with a 10-inch bread knife and we were locked in the bathroom hiding from her while the police were called. After that I felt too unsafe to stay. So that night I took the duvet cover off the bed and got a train into the city. I didn't know where to go or what I would do when I got there and that's how I ended up homeless.

I got to the station really late at night. There was a station cleaner, and he obviously saw that I was really young, so he showed me where I could sleep in the station and not get kicked out by security. He showed me a hiding place on one of the platforms, told me how I had to duck down and hide so nobody would see me. On my first night I slept there, and he woke me up at 6 o'clock in the morning with a doughnut and a cup of tea and told me to make a run for it before the security came and saw me. I've never forgotten his kindness.

Some of the kindest things I've ever experienced were on the streets. But often it would be the complete opposite and I'd be so invisible that people wouldn't even acknowledge me. Sometimes I used to play a game, when I was bored, where I used to ask people the time, and nobody would stop and nobody would tell me what the time was. Because I was sitting in a doorway and they assumed I was asking them for money. I would be spat on. I know people who were pissed on in the middle of the night by people who were drunk. The level of violence was so extreme. There was one night when I was badly attacked, and I was just running and running, and I went and hid under the phone boxes. I was just wearing a t-shirt covered in blood and it was so obvious I'd been raped. But the police told me, 'You can't sleep here,' and they escorted me off to the station. I think in that moment all I needed was for one of them to have turned around and asked, 'What has happened to you?' and I would have told them. But I didn't tell anyone what had happened to me because I was too frightened. I knew after that I couldn't ever turn to the police for any kind of protection or help. Looking back, I find it really hard to understand how the police can do that to a young girl who has clearly been sexually assaulted. I needed help so badly and I was lying underneath the phone box half dressed, badly beaten up and with blood all over me.

I used to go to the Homeless Persons Unit every single morning and they used to tell me, 'You are not vulnerable enough; you are not in priority need.' I got told, 'You have been on the streets too long; you don't have mental health problems; you don't have drug and alcohol problems; you haven't been in prison; you don't meet any of our criteria.' I went to the Homeless Persons Unit after I'd been raped. I was really vulnerable and at that point I was sleeping rough by myself. I wasn't taking drugs, but I still wasn't ok.

I just acclimatised to street life really quickly. You find something on the streets that kind of keeps you there and even if you are not dragged into those spirals of alcohol and drug addiction, it is almost like that belonging and community make it hard to leave. It's heart-breaking; you are seeing people get worse and worse. We weren't thriving at all, we were just destroying ourselves and yet we still stayed there. I don't know why.

I think choice is the wrong word. I think when people say you 'make a choice' to be homeless it is really dangerous, because I don't think anyone chooses to be homeless. People end up homeless and once you are on the streets, it's not a choice to stay there, because saying 'a choice' is giving the impression that you can do something about it if you want to. When you are that battered down, you start to believe what is around you. You start to believe that you are worthless, you are dirty, and this is the only place you belong. You start to believe you don't really have a future and you lose any sense of hope. It's not that easy to make a decision that this isn't going to be my life anymore. Where do you start? I couldn't turn to any authorities and say, 'Look, I want to get off the streets. Help me,' because they were saying, 'You are fine, you are ok, you are surviving.'

When you're homeless and you're with a lot of other people who are in the same situation as you are, and you've come from a background where you haven't really felt any belonging or sense of family before, it is like the street becomes your family. Sometimes on the street I felt so safe and looked after and protected by the people I was with. Yet at the same time, it was so unsafe, and I was so vulnerable. So even though I thought people were my friends and felt protected by them, I also got into a lot of bad situations that way.

Jessica

Drugs, alcohol and mental health were massive issues. I remember my friend being unconscious on the steps after a heroin overdose. There were so many people walking past and I was begging them to stop and help, but nobody would call an ambulance for him. I lost a lot of friends on the streets. My friend Ronny went down to Brighton and died of a heroin overdose there. I never saw him again. I had another friend who died of a heart attack and he was only twenty-seven. The situation we were in was so desperate and it was really easy to be drawn into drugs. I feel lucky that I never became an addict. I messed around a bit, but I was never an addict. But most of the people I was with were and their lives were completely destroyed. There are very few people I know from that time who got out of it. Most of them have died, or they are still there. It breaks my heart. It's the horror of it—being sixteen and seeing a friend with a needle hanging out of their arm. Having friends collapsed in the doorway and trying to wake them up. Seeing the violence that drink does. I remember there was a massive fight between two street people and just seeing this guy lying there in a pool of blood. Sometimes it was literally a case of kill or be killed. There was a really awful incident when I was on the streets, where a couple of people were murdered in their sleeping bags by a man who was drunk coming out of the clubs. I heard of people setting fire to sleeping bags while someone was inside. There was violence everywhere, within the street community and then from members of the public too. There was no escaping it.

The way people judge you on the streets is really hard. It's like you are a piece of dirt. People walk past you and tell you to 'get a job'. Being a woman, you are so vulnerable to men, who think that just because you're homeless you'll do anything for a couple of quid. You see the worst side of people and from people you wouldn't expect it from. Like the middle-class businessman who has been to the pub with his mates and thinks it's funny to insult a homeless girl. Or a group of drunk college lads who think it's funny to urinate on somebody they see asleep in a fire exit. I'm not sure what it is that people see when they see someone sleeping rough, because often it seems to bring out the worst in people.

I had two separate experiences of being homeless. The second time was after I became really unwell. It felt much worse the second time. It wasn't as brutal, but it was worse. I was completely on my own and I was a lot more scared. I guess I had all the memories from being homeless before and was still so traumatised. So, the second time, instead of sleeping in doorways, I would wander aimlessly all night, or I'd go into 24-hour cafes and sit there by myself.

I think the difference was that the second time I didn't trust anyone, so I wouldn't talk to anyone. I was so ill, and they discharged me straight from hospital onto the streets. I was so depressed, I could hardly function and could barely get myself through a day. I was completely invisible in homelessness. I didn't walk around with a sleeping bag like I had when I was younger and no one who saw me would have known I was homeless at all. I didn't experience the same level of violence, or stigma and discrimination, I was just completely invisible.

It was so desperate, and it felt like there weren't any options. The Homeless Persons Unit still wouldn't help me because, again, I wasn't considered in 'priority need', but I don't know how much more vulnerable I could have been. I had nowhere to go at all. The ironic thing is that, although the council were telling me I was 'not a priority', a lot of the hostels and night shelters were saying I couldn't have a bed there, as my 'support needs were too high'. When I look back, if somebody had helped me the first time I was on the streets, aged sixteen, then I don't think I'd have ended up homeless again. It was the emotional impact of those first years sleeping rough and all the trauma I experienced that led to me becoming so unwell.

Jessica

NOT IN PRIORITY NEED
ANONYMOUS

Using anonymised mental health notes, this is a timeline of one young woman's experience trying to get help for mental health difficulties while homeless. Lisa's* experience is of being passed from one service to another over a number of years, while her mental health worsened, eventually resulting in being sectioned under the Mental Health Act. Lisa writes:

My difficulties go back to early childhood. I was diagnosed with Developmental Delay aged three years old. I was very anxious as a child and I was selectively mute for many years, refusing to talk to anyone outside of my family. Looking back, I think I was too terrified to speak. I was being sexually abused.

Throughout childhood and adolescence I remained painfully shy, had extreme social anxiety and found social interaction and social communication extremely difficult. I was finally diagnosed with Asperger's Syndrome/'High-functioning Autism' in my late teens at a specialist autism clinic. However, the clinic offered a diagnostic assessment only, so I never received any autism-specific support.

I left home at the age of fifteen. I was housed briefly by social services in a hostel for young people transitioning from care. In this hostel I was attacked and felt too frightened to stay. I then ended up on the streets.

I have decided to share brief extracts from my mental health notes, to show how difficult it is as a young person to get access to housing and mental health support.

* Lisa is a pseudonym — identifying details (including age) have been changed to protect Lisa's identity. Information has also been removed to protect the identity of professionals who have written these notes. Therefore, at times, notes have been adjusted slightly, but otherwise remain true to the original content. This is based on a real account of one woman's journey through the mental health system.

NOT IN PRIORITY NEED

AGE 17

•

I was referred to an Eating Disorders Unit by a support worker while living in a short-stay hostel for vulnerable young women.

Unit Manager
Eating Disorders Unit

Lisa has been a resident at the hostel for the past four months. She was referred to outreach services following a chequered history of rough sleeping. She left home at the age of fifteen after a breakdown in the relationship with her family. She has a history of significant childhood trauma and sexual abuse and recently while sleeping rough on the streets she was raped. Lisa has recently expressed a desire in gaining support in coming to terms with these issues and has looked into individual counselling and psychotherapy options available to her.

Compounded by the above Lisa has battled with recurring Anorexia Nervosa since her early teens. This has presented as very erratic eating patterns or starvation and she currently remains underweight according to standardised height/weight ratios. She also suffers from severe depression and occasional incidents of deliberate self-harm. The latter have taken form as cutting to both her arms. Up until this time she has not consulted with any specialist services although maintaining acute awareness of her situation and insight into the roots of her difficulties.

The Eating Disorders Unit didn't respond to the referral and I wasn't offered an assessment.

ANONYMOUS

AGE 18

·

The second attempt to get help was from an NHS psychotherapy service for young people. I made a self-referral.

Assessment report:

When I collected her from the waiting room I found
a thin, painfully shy and rather unhealthy looking
girl. She has long stringy black hair, her skin looks
pale, she was dressed in clean but old and worn out
looking clothes and her Doc Marten boots were
split open at the seams. It seemed more appropriate
to offer her a nourishing meal than offer her an
appointment for psychotherapy.

I would go to my therapy sessions with my sleeping bag and belongings and then leave fifty minutes later with nowhere to go.

End of term report:

The issue of her homelessness has to be constantly
addressed as it tends to emerge throughout all her
material. She did manage to move out of the hostel
(where two people died while she was there) into
shared supported housing but she left that place
after her room was broken into and she was burgled.

Not feeling that it was safe to return there she
again became homeless. While she seems to find it
impossible to find a safe place to live, she also
realises that the streets (which once offered
a haven of sorts) are not a safe place for her
to be either.

A few months later I was raped by a group of five men. It was the second time I'd been raped on the streets. My mental health deteriorated significantly.

NOT IN PRIORITY NEED

End of term report:

Lisa has described in a number of sessions that it
is harder and harder for her to hold on and that she
might kill herself. She knows she places herself at
great risk in these states but feels she is powerless
to stop them from taking over. She continues to cut
herself and while she has always been very thin she
is now alarmingly thin and looks terribly under-
nourished. I have been increasingly concerned about
her state and asked her to see a psychiatrist in our
department who was also worried about her and thought
an in-patient admission would be appropriate. Both
of us were concerned about her extreme thinness.
However, I am uncertain about the feasibility
of psychotherapy continuing as she is homeless again
and it is unlikely the trust will renew her contract
for treatment as she is not within the catchment
area, due to no fixed abode.

Because I had no fixed address my funding for therapy ended.
I wasn't offered any follow-up support.

AGE 19
•

I would use a homeless day centre to have a shower, store
my belongings and get cheap meals. I had an assessment with
one of their support workers. She wrote to adult social services
to try and request an urgent community care assessment:

To whom it may concern:

I am writing in regard to a young woman who has
recently come to the attention of our organisation.
She has a diagnosis of Asperger's syndrome. Lisa
explained that she has been living on the streets
for some time and is homeless. Her condition has
an effect on her understanding of communication and
although she may appear high functioning this aspect

of her condition creates great difficulties for her in social interaction, which in turn makes her vulnerable and at risk. She finds it hard to cope in new situations and speaking to people she does not know is a traumatising situation for her as she has to struggle to understand the meaning of what is being said to her. Her current circumstance of being homeless is compounding feelings of isolation, depression and stress.

I am writing to request that Lisa has an assessment of need under the Community Care Act as her needs appear quite high and represent a real barrier to her ability to live independently. A thorough assessment would establish her level of need. Lisa needs support to find a home.

I had a community care assessment through adult social services. As my diagnosis was Asperger's syndrome/autistic spectrum they referred me to their Learning Disability Service, but since I don't have a learning disability the referral was closed with no action taken.

AGE 20
•

My GP wrote the following letter to the Community Mental Health Team:

I would be most grateful if you could see this young woman who has just registered with our practice. She was diagnosed with Asperger's syndrome in her teens, by a clinical psychologist at a specialist autism service. Apparently, this was a diagnosis assessment only.

She would greatly appreciate some long-term ongoing therapy, particularly in terms of social skills and interpersonal relationships. She finds it almost impossible to maintain eye contact, she is very

NOT IN PRIORITY NEED

nervous and fidgety, and she is overrun with worry
about social interaction. Lisa was sexually abused
as a child and has suffered from periods of Anorexia
since her teens. She has spent the last four years
homeless, mostly sleeping rough. She occasionally
stays with a friend in our practice area.

I was referred to a day hospital. This was my first experience of
being in adult psychiatric services. The day hospital did their best
to support me in accessing housing. This is what they wrote to the
Homeless Person's Unit:

HOW IS PRESENT HOUSING UNSATISFACTORY?
(e.g. overcrowding/mobility problems)

    No fixed abode
   → Negative impact on mental state,
      which is now deteriorating further

SPECIAL HOUSING NEEDS (if any)

    * Needs stable place to live
    * Currently very vulnerable due
      to fragile mental state

ADDITIONAL INFORMATION (if any e.g. social history)

    * Previously assaulted when homeless
    * Currently receiving treatment for
      low mood as a day patient at
      ██████████████ day hospital
    * On medication

I was found not to be 'in priority need' by the Homeless
Person's Unit.

ANONYMOUS

AGE 21

·

At this point I started to lose hope and could no longer cope with my situation. I was referred to a crisis house. The maximum stay was twenty-eight days.

Re: Lisa (No Fixed Abode)

Lisa was referred to the project by the day hospital as they had noticed she was experiencing feelings of hopelessness and suicidal thoughts. Lisa was homeless, and this contributed to these feelings.

Lisa was self-harming as a means of coping with her feelings. She had thoughts of taking an overdose. Staff at the day hospital thought her condition had been deteriorating lately. They were concerned about her mental state since she became homeless again. She had also seen a man from her past on the streets who she thought had died some years ago from a heroin overdose. Upon seeing this man Lisa became very depressed due to a past history of this man having raped her previously.

Lisa was very concerned about her housing issues and being homeless. Staff wrote letters to the Homeless Person's Unit and also gave her forms for two different supported housing organisations. Lisa promptly filled in the forms and they were sent off.

Lisa spent most evenings trying to sell 'The Big Issue'. With staff support she was able to apply for Employment Support Allowance. As the end of her stay approached she became more anxious and unsettled as she was worried about sleeping rough again. The night before she was due to leave she admitted to staff that she had taken a significant overdose of paracetamol and anti-depressants in an attempt to end her life. She was taken to A&E by ambulance and able to leave hospital once medically cleared.

NOT IN PRIORITY NEED

AGE 23

•

I was still in and out of hostels or sleeping rough. I ended up attempting suicide several more times and was sectioned under the Mental Health Act on a Section 3.

Delete the indents not applicable

I am of the opinion that it is necessary

    (i)   in the interests of the patient's own health

    (ii)   in the interests of the patient's own safety

    ~~(iii) with a view to the protection of other persons~~

that this patient should receive treatment and it cannot be provided unless he/she is detained under Section 3 of the Act, for the following reasons:

(Reasons should indicate whether other methods of care or treatment [e.g. out-patient treatment or local services authority services] are available and if so why they are not appropriate and why informal admission is not appropriate)

    (1)   High risk of suicidal act

    (2)   Risk of absconding if voluntary patient very high

    (3)   No other suitable/safe options to supervise/keep her safe at this point

Sometime later I was discharged from the Section 3 but remained extremely unwell.

In total I spent seven years homeless, mostly sleeping on the street. Eventually I was offered a place in supported housing and then got my council flat. But by that time I'd attempted suicide twelve times and had several psychiatric admissions. I had to become that unwell to be considered 'vulnerable enough' and 'in priority need'.

ANONYMOUS

← N

7
·
WHERE I SLEPT
LAST NIGHT:
Under Charing Cross Bridge

BEKKI PERRIMAN

INTERVIEW
Nikki

I am twenty-two and living on the streets and it's hard. Everybody just looks at you as if to go, 'Are you even old enough to be on the streets?' I was put into care from when I was eleven, right up until I was seventeen. So, I've pretty much done this my whole life. I used to go and beg for food from my neighbours when I was a kid cos my dad didn't care about me and they kicked me out of home by the time I was eleven. When I left care, I was living with my boyfriend and we got into rent arrears and the landlord wouldn't let us pay off instalments, so we ended up on the streets.

I went to the council and I said, 'I'm homeless, could you please help me?', and they said, 'Oh no, go to the homeless advice centre,' and then the homeless advice centre tell me, 'Oh no you need to go to the council,' and I was like, 'They tell me to come here and you are telling me to go there,' and I hate it. Especially when they tell you to get rid of your dog before they want to house you and that is one thing that I will not do is get rid of my dog. Apparently there is supposed to be dog friendly hostels and hotels, but I don't know where they are; I've never been able to find them.

Some people don't like you having a dog. The looks that you get. Yesterday a guy said to me, 'You shouldn't have a dog, that's terrible,' and I was like, 'Sorry, I can't help being homeless.' But a lot of people do have sympathy for you. This woman heard him and so she walked up and handed me a tenner and she said, 'It's hard being where you are and hopefully this helps you and your dog,' and I said, 'Thank you, it does.'

I've noticed it's the people who don't have money who are the ones that give it away and it's the ones that have money that don't like to give it away. Although I have had some people help me out. A lot of people buy me food and all that, and it's good, because at least I'm not actually going hungry and I've got food for the dog as well. She's always getting treats. Yesterday, two wee boys came up to me and went, 'Here's two tins of dog food and a cheeseburger for you.' I took one bite out of the cheeseburger and gave her the rest. There are days where I'll get an appetite and days where I go hungry because of the situation I'm in. You do get days where you'll not eat and there's days where you cannot be bothered to eat.

I used to sound better than this and it's actually ruined my voice. It's given me a really bad chest infection and I think I've got pleurisy in my lungs because of it. What I mean is that I've got liquid in my lungs that I'm trying to get out.

My dog sleeps in beside me so she's wrapped up. She's in with me, so I'm safe that way. Also, I've got my fiancé as well, who keeps me protected. The only person I've got in my life is my fiancé. He is the only person that does care for me. I don't want to ever lose him. If you are in a relationship they should be able to house the two of you instead of going, 'No, only one of you is being housed and the other one has to stay on the streets.' That's the way it is, because they don't like housing couples and I don't know why.

Emotionally, I do get grumpy quite a lot. If I'm not feeling too good, I'm biting my man's head off all the time and I don't want to fall out with him because of it. But I think it's the stage where it's going to happen, because of the situation I'm in, and I don't want that happening.

If I had a house, I would get breakfast, have a coffee, tidy up and then take the dog for a walk in the park. I don't really have a daily routine anymore because of my situation. My daily routine is to just sit and beg and make money. I've got about five pitches. Sometimes there are arguments over pitches. I did have one guy who said, 'Well, that's my pitch,' and I said, 'You can go away because I am sitting there.' If you go onto somebody's pitch and sit there, sometimes they will tell you to move and you tell them, 'I was sitting here first.' Sometimes they'll try and get their pitches back off you and I tell them, 'No, you are not getting it, it's mine.'

I used to take drugs quite a lot, so it's screwed with my head. You've heard of those legal highs, haven't you? I used to smoke them constantly. You see, synthetic cannabis, it's a million times stronger than normal cannabis. Spice, Exodus, Annihilation, there's that many of them I can't really say — Very Bomb, Cherry Bomb, The Joker, Pandora's Box … There's so many of them out there — Clockwork Orange, K2 Black … My old man, he took a heart attack from legal highs and he still smokes them. It just makes me go to sleep. Literally, it calms me down and I sit there for forty-five minutes and go to sleep, wake up, take another bong, go to sleep for another forty-five minutes. It's very, very addictive and it's very dangerous to actually smoke. People go, 'What are you smoking

Nikki

that for? It kills you,' and I say, 'It's not killed me yet and I'll smoke it until it does.' I didn't care if it killed me, but I'm still here five years later.

I would just sit on my pitch, smoking legal highs so I could go to sleep after begging for money. I've got to be honest, yes, sometimes the money was for legal highs and sometimes it was for food. It's not just the legal highs, it goes on me and the dog and food for her as well, so she is getting something out of it too.

I stopped smoking legal highs when I found out I was pregnant. I haven't registered with a doctor yet, so I need to do that, register with a doctor and go and have a scan. But it's horrible finding out you are pregnant, and you've got nowhere to go. I only just found out, literally a few days ago. I was shocked, totally shocked and gobsmacked. I was happy too, as I've always wanted a child, but I didn't want one right now. I wanted to get sorted with a house and stuff first and then try. But it's too late now and this wee one will be mine for the rest of my life and so I'm happy about it. Scared, but happy.

Nikki

HOW TO ~~MAKE ART~~ LISTEN
IN A HOUSING CRISIS
JANNA GRAHAM

In recent years, questions about the role of art within the current crisis of housing have been in high circulation: echoing in the halls of grass-roots organisations, real estate developers, art schools, charities and urban planners alike. Some people within this discussion suggest that artists and art institutions are best suited to generating visions for the future of local areas. People who follow this train of thought, like *Guardian* writer Jonathan Jones, argue that the changes artists bring to neighbourhoods and to visions of improvement are inherently good, that artists bring 'culture' to an area,[1] or at the very least are innocent of any complicity with the process of displacement that is at the core of 'redevelopment' initiatives. Others suggest that, intended or not, artists in this context are directly involved in the erasure of local forms of cultural expression and life that do not conform to dominant regeneration aesthetics. In many cases the future visions they produce or solicit from community members are already written by developers and local councils. The artist is understood here as an asset to private/public housing partnerships in duping residents into participatory 'visioning' exercises that in the end, and often unbeknown to them, legitimise the process through which working-class residents are erased from the areas where they live. My own experiences of these processes are that councils and developers like artists and curators to be involved in presenting artistic and curatorial 'visions' in order to erase what to them appear as the unattractive look and feel of working-class, migrant and unhoused community residents, to treat neighbourhoods like blank canvases upon which to imagine futures in the absence of the diversity and complex lives of the people who live in them, and to enlist those with the most to lose in tokenistic forms of participation in this process. It is through such 'visions' that people who don't fit the pre-fabricated models of concrete parks, quirkily crafted buildings and sterile landscape gardening, are rendered invisible and inaudible even before they are forced to leave by evictions, demolitions and rampant policing.

Beyond its capacity to imagine and envision, the current housing establishment's interest in artistic and curatorial processes runs even deeper. These processes are attractive because they mimic the art world's own contradictory formation: its production of class hierarchies and intense elitism, while at the same time 'reaching out' through community engagement to 'poor communities', ensuring all the while that such poor communities remain docile in the face of the violent forces wreaked on them by the very same elites who frequent, donate and sit on the boards of directors of art galleries. That these activities are irreconcilable

JANNA GRAHAM

and at the same time never come into conflict is what makes the arts most attractive to developers and planners.

In spite of the emphasis on the visual in this process of envisioning, questions of voicing — who is heard and how — are increasingly prevalent. People are recorded, testimonies taken, stories extracted and circulated, but often at the hands of artists and developers and not in the service of the broader housing struggle of the people who bear the brunt of de-housing processes. What does it mean to make struggles with housing visible and audible in a context in which artists, developers, journalists and social researchers increasingly mobilise strategies of participation, 'giving voice' and 'making visible' to extract value for personal or speculative profit?

On the other hand, what can it mean to make audible — to *hear* — the experiences of those in the best position to articulate that the real housing crisis lies not in a lack of housing per se, but in state sponsored, speculatively oriented and socially supported acts of social cleansing? How can practices of listening based in the complexity of situated experiences of a crisis strategically produced by the agents of speculative profit (including those elected to represent us) enable a continual process of political analysis and struggle against it?

The Doorways Project works on these questions, attempting to analyse the ramifications of complex modes of housing precarity from the experience of those who feel its most violent effects. Beginning from the intersections of lives lived, it exposes the fraying seams of a social world that seeks to naturalise and neutralise relations of domination, experienced most acutely by the unhoused and rough-sleeping residents — yes *residents* — of our communities. Those quoted within this book describe both the failure of services and the barbed violence of forces that conspire to dis-place and keep them out of housing, safety and support, but also make clear that the housing crisis is a social crisis that cannot be solved by public/private housing partnerships, squiggly buildings and the like. They expose that this crisis is produced precisely in the name of an aesthetic and a mode of speculation designed to wage war on the poor, the troubled, the precarious, in the name of profit for the few. As such, the project poses questions to practices of cultural production beyond how we produce without being complicit in the process of speculative real estate development, and suggests the wholesale inadequacy of most mainstream modes of making and producing art in responding to the complex conditions of precarity in our time.

HOW TO ~~MAKE ART~~ LISTEN
IN A HOUSING CRISIS

OF VOICING
AND VANISHING

'It was scary, really scary. I actually lost my voice.
I had laryngitis, I think, and so I couldn't speak
and I had no voice at all.'
– Arna

In her interview for The Doorways Project Arna speaks of a
voicelessness that is physical: what happens when cold, weary
nights, absolute exposure and fear convene to fail vocal chords.
She speaks of a moment where the worst kind of recurring dream
is realised, of being threatened, attacked and totally unable
to speak. Her discussion of voicelessness is both her own and
an amplification of the otherwise unheard experience of an
increasing number of people for whom life is regularly threatened
by the absence of a social framework that values common
resources for all.

In most urban contexts today, this silencing or vanishing
of voices is the end effect of the narrative of inevitable progress
that underpins policies of planning, development and privatisation.
Within this narrative, those who stand in the way of unstoppable
improvement, of a city moving towards 'the light', remain as
visible reminders of the violence of this force of the inevitable.
'They' who do not fit, who stand in the path, must be removed,
ignored and pushed to its edges. They are relegated to the cultures
of the failed, the past, the shadow figures or the disappearing—
those who, structurally and physically, cannot speak. They are
marked by the empty sleeping bags we see in alleys, the endless
washing to keep the doorways' occupants away, the spiked benches
and the silence of passers by. London-based group Southwark Notes,
composed of local people using research and artistic/creative
processes (graphics, direct action) in their struggles against the
gentrification of the Elephant and Castle neighbourhood, have
analysed this in great detail. They suggest that the very term
'regeneration' works in conjunction with broader tactics of what
Lauren Berlant describes as 'hygienic governmentality',[2] a kind
of social cleansing, directed at the displacement of working-class
communities. They describe the mythic representations of council
tenants, social housing and the unhoused that precede and continue
throughout the development process through which governments
and developers cultivate 'the unlovable modern demons of the
underclass—fatty single mothers of three, skinny junkies lurking

JANNA GRAHAM

on the landings, professional claimants living it up', which 'enables the Council to displace its own brutality onto a supposed demand from a mythical general public to "sort it out"'.[3] These images mask the other side: intentionally run-down services, strategically broken-down communities and uninhabitable architectures, to produce what Christopher Jones describes as the double helix of justification 'suggesting that the project of housing and communities produced under the principle of common resources, are a failure, full of crime and anti-social behaviour; necessitating "revitalisation"'.[4] Forced instability here is used to legitimise the disappearing rather than to contend with it through common solutions. Here, the making of people's precarity is not only a condition of life's increasingly insecure circumstances but, in writer Isabell Lorey's words, a 'category of order' that makes hierarchies through which certain people appear as social 'others'. This way of segmenting society provides a cover for and distraction from the 'naturalized relations of domination', that underpin processes like speculative real estate development and de-funding of services.[5]

As Arna's statements make clear, and as the countless stories of other orators in The Doorways Project make visceral, the narratives of both precarious lives and the 'hygienic govern-mentality' manifest simultaneously in a voicelessness and a violence directed at those who do not fit the image of the new from both the authorities and many users of the city, whose abuse of those seen to be undesirable is in effect legitimised by the state and the housing industrial complex. The silence of unhoused residents is not accidental or due to an individual failure of voice, but structurally produced and socially enforced.

On the other hand, artistic attempts at voicing this silence cannot be read as completely innocent. Artists, poets and other cultural workers have always played a role in voicing the lives of those thrown to the edges of what is seen, by those in power, to be the inevitable force of progress. In the colonial Canadian context, from which we can draw some parallels to the ways in which cities are currently developed, the theft of land and resources from indigenous people was accompanied by images of the impossible lives of indigenous communities and narratives of a people already 'doomed'. These narratives and their accom-panying visual culture were used to both imagine and legitimise the 'vanishing' of people upon whose land colonial governments and settler corporations hoped to profit. Artists 'gave voice' to those who did not fit the development narrative as a way

HOW TO ~~MAKE ART~~ LISTEN
IN A HOUSING CRISIS

of showing respect for their soon-to-be-lost cultures. But, at the same time, they were solidifying and naturalising the idea of disappearance that was at play in the violence of dispossession. As colonial governments knew at the time (hence their commissioning of many such projects), the participation of artists was essential in sensitising various publics to a plight constructed wholly by colonial authorities. Images, texts and acts of voicing rendered the violent process of extraction of indigenous commons sympathetic, natural and even beautiful in its tragedy. Artists seen merely as innocent observers, lending voice and visibility to those at the sad end of the process, were supportive but not *involved*. The dynamic between voicing and disappearing served multiple aims, covering over the image of local residents fighting back or resisting, and convincing incoming occupants that they were neither complicit nor culpable in the process of displacement and, in many cases, of murder.[6]

In urban neighbourhoods in the UK, community voicing initiatives around redevelopment, like these colonial artistic visions, can extract and distract voices, while at the same time producing the very conditions of silence they are designed to overcome. Recourse to 'memory work' and 'voicing' projects is often the first response to conflict in urban neighbourhoods resisting gentrification in the UK. Council- or developer-hired community engagement artists enlist people in projects to hear the stories of 'vanishing' or 'silent' local residents, at the same time as they are vanishing and silencing them. Voices of protest, agony, the anger or the pain of displacement, of precarious and impossible housing, cannot be heard, as the relationship between silencing and 'giving voice' is produced by propagators of housing and social precarity, the ones who dis-place, erase, evict and fail to hear in the first place.

Less sinister but equally ill conceived are voicing projects undertaken by artists and researchers who take such voices and present them in other contexts disconnected from struggle — universities, art galleries and so on — into worlds where notions of authenticity and urgency add value for those who extract them, propelling cultural and intellectual capital with little to no effect on the sites where vanishing and silencing take place, or on the lives of those affected. Here lies a struggle between those who seek to be heard and the mechanics of voicing, which seems to always require an interlocutor, a more powerful figure, organisation, researcher or force focused on victimhood, and cannot hear collective responses to the intentional social war waged against the marginalised. This amplification of the voices of 'vanishing people', like the running down of buildings, is used as the justification for the next steps of privatisation, de-housing, eviction, demolition and social cleansing.

In this landscape of voicing and vanishing, how can the process at play in The Doorways Project be heard?

A VOICE AND
SOMETHING MORE

While cultural and political organising commonly prioritise the act of voicing, what The Doorways Project does most potently is to question what it is to listen to the housing crisis. This call to listen poses significant questions to the fields of cultural work and political organising. While within these circuits we might hear of a project like this one referred to in terms of 'voicing' or 'empowerment', The Doorways Project makes every attempt not to fetishise the speaking of 'disadvantaged' or 'vulnerable' people, nor does it legitimise the vanishing or rest satisfied with a modicum of consciousness raising. It calls to a kind of listening that hears and aligns with an emerging analysis of those in struggle, fragmented, pained and deeply precarious as they may be. As its curator suggests, 'The direct voice, apart from asserting its human presence, enables listeners to connect on a personal level and enter the speaker's world of experience.'

Read less through the frameworks of participatory arts and research and more as analysis from below of those at the sharpest edge of the housing struggle, listening to The Doorways Project interviews in the doorways where their occupants are regularly silenced and 'vanished' suggests that we listen differently. What we hear is that what is often described as a crisis of housing or homelessness is in fact a war waged against the poor and precarious, which takes place on many levels simultaneously: the corporate speculation that generates a scarcity of affordable places to live; a discriminatory health care system that cannot cope with complex mental health issues; the ongoing culture of misogyny that legitimises threats to women's safety both on the street and in the shelters and charities set up to support them.

This articulation of the complex precarity of unhoused residents heard in these doorways de-naturalises the centrally constructed narrative of the housing crisis, and the order of things that renders unhoused people socially 'other'. The intersecting

HOW TO ~~MAKE ART~~ LISTEN
IN A HOUSING CRISIS

failures experienced by unhoused people profoundly bring into question the mantra that the only solution to the housing crisis is more private housing. It asks us to remember Audre Lorde's call to intersectional approaches, that there 'is no such thing as a single-issue struggle because we do not live single-issue lives'.[7] It calls to us to attend to life as a common set of circumstances, to trace these experiences through systems in crisis and to imagine other ways of organising life.

The Doorways Project, then, is a call to listen. As such, it also exposes glimmers through the experiences of complex precarity articulated by unhoused residents in the technologies of kindness, commoning and survival that are learned in the community who experience it at its most dire edges. What listening to The Doorways Project exposes is both precarity in its most fundamental, bare forms of violence, but also in its intelligence, its provocation that we move away from what Judith Butler calls an 'ontology of individualism' and towards ways of being in collective and common life.[8] Here there is also a call to the practices of cultural organisation, asking us to listen and act upon what is heard in the sites through which the regular processes of vanishing and silencing take place.

LISTENING BEYOND

If not giving voice, and not (only) making art, what is it to foster listening to the housing crisis?

A first answer to this question is that fostering listening is not simply that of 'giving voice', 'making visible' or 'giving a platform to' those most affected by the crisis of speculative real estate development. This 'giving voice' or, in more cynical readings, 'extracting voice' for one's own artistic or institutional value production, must be recontextualised as a call to listen.

This places responsibility onto cultural organisations and cultural organisers to create contexts where the experiences of people can be heard in their multiplicity, and indeed in which what is heard or voiced can be acted upon.

The Doorways Project calls out for such a context for listening, but this call, one hears, has not been fully met in the current cultural milieu. A security guard cares for the technical aspects of the project but is untouched by hearing the stories of unhoused residents, continuing to clean the steps to stave off the 'undesirable' others that he assumes (and not incorrectly) are

JANNA GRAHAM

directly opposed by the aesthetic regimes of contemporary art. This institutional image, of one hand holding the amplifier and the other holding the broom of social cleansing, is emblematic of a problem in mainstream cultural production that I recognise from many years of working as a curator in art galleries. The image speaks less of the ignorance of an individual guard, who is no doubt steeped in his own set of circumstances in the web of precarity, and more of the impossible contradictions that lie at the heart of a mode of cultural production that orients itself around the voice and 'making visible' over questions of commitment, collective organisation, antagonism and consequence. A focus on listening attunes to the experiences and analyses with collective political and social struggles for housing as a right—both within the operating practices of institutions and in the world beyond their doors.

To produce a context for listening is not only to ensure that the audio equipment is in operation (though this is very important and often not bothered with in projects developed by the socially marginalised, as opposed to those for international art stars), or that brochures promote the event or that catalogue essays are written, but suggest the importance of taking a side, joining the struggle for the communalisation of housing and other social services, in order to foster an environment for listening that facilitates a sense of responsibility towards those whose voices are newly heard, and to the unforeseeable ends they might imagine together. It is to be well versed and situated enough in political struggle and strategy so as to hear the beginnings of organisational processes as they emerge and to support and resource them accordingly. It is to be committed to and knowledgeable in the technicalities of the redistribution of cultural resources (money, spaces, platforms, cultural capital) so as to support the actions that emerge from those who have listened together. It is to antagonise the property developers and speculators who sit on the boards of universities and cultural institutions and it is, finally and literally, to let go as and when those engaged in a process of listening suggest that it is time to do so.

Here, listening is not a fetish but a praxis (theory + practice)—a praxis that asks that we follow through on what is heard and do not simply stage it. To reorganise cultural resources around listening in the current climate would be profound and profoundly resistant. It would ask that we take the question of precarious life and housing within it as an urgent call to action and not a motif, a problem to be worked on and not a theme; it

HOW TO ~~MAKE ART~~ LISTEN
IN A HOUSING CRISIS

would ask that we listen in order to understand what is common across our differences of experience and to produce what Isabell Lorey calls 'communities of care'.

Listening to The Doorways Project demonstrates that the modes of presentation available to us are small and marginal in the face of the enormity of what we have heard. We hear the need for a kind of cultural organising that profoundly intersects with various practices of life-making, that desegregates categories like 'housing', 'mental health' and 'culture' to create radical groups and lives prepared and resourced to fight against forces of speculation, vanishing, social cleansing, individualisation and othering.

The Doorways Project is one step along this path that asks us to listen for a future where this fight is no longer as necessary as it is today.

1 JONATHAN JONES, 'Artwashing: The New Watchword for Anti-gentrification', *The Guardian* (18 July 2016), available at www.theguardian.com.
2 LAUREN BERLANT, *The Queen of America Goes to Washington City* (Durham: Duke University Press, 1997), p. 175; emphasis mine.
3 CHRISTOPHER JONES, 'Pyramid Dead — The Artangel of History', *Mute* (17 April 2014), available at www.metamute.org/editorial/articles/pyramid-dead-artangel-history.
4 Ibid.
5 ISABELL LOREY, 'Governmental Precarization', trans. Aileen Derieg, *eipcp.net* (January 2011), available at http://eipcp.net/transversal/0811/lorey/en.

6 DANIEL FRANCIS, *The Imaginary Indian: The Image of The Indian in Canadian Culture* (Vancouver: Arsenal Pulp Press, 1992).
7 AUDRE LORDE, *Sister Outsider: Essays and Speeches by Audre Lorde* (Berkeley: Crossing Press, 2007), pp. 134–44.
8 JUDITH BUTLER, 'Precarious Life, Grievable Life', in *Frames of War: When Is Life Grievable?* (London: Verso, 2009), p. 23.

JANNA GRAHAM

TWO REFLECTIONS ON
ART AND NEOLIBERALISM
SHIRI SHALMY and
ANDREA LUKA ZIMMERMAN

TAKING SIDES
•
SHIRI SHALMY

I cannot write about The Doorways Project without considering
my own motivation in curating it. My collaboration with Bekki
is the longest and most meaningful professional relationship I've
had with an artist throughout my career as a curator and producer.

We first worked together in 2013, when I curated a
London art festival, which awarded Bekki a small solo exhibition
in a disused office. It was her first public show. We then went
on to apply for a couple of grants, which funded the development
and production of The Doorways Project touring exhibition, and
this book.

I am interested in the tension between the expectation
and the futility of art as a medium and a practice to affect social
and political change. In my view, art production (and we should
be honest about the process when we, otherwise, talk about an
'art industry') under capitalism is not different from other forms
of production, which involve the balancing of capital, labour and
value. Like other forms of capitalist production, it also involves
extraction, exploitation and alienation.

While acknowledging a tradition of political art, from
Guernica to the Situationists, from murals to Punk, I would
suggest that providing a critique of capitalism is not the same
as working outside or against it. The successfully hegemonic
nature of capitalism means that all our relationships, far beyond
just financial transactions, have been monetised, and that our
imagination is a mere reflection of these interactions. Currently,
there is no place outside capitalism.

Responding to the desolation of the Thatcher years, New
Labour's cultural strategies around participation, inclusion and
diversity—backed by significant public funding—resulted in the
notion that the very act of 'engagement' is in itself a (sanctioned)
form of political critique and, indeed, a solution to social problems.
That representation, based on categories such as gender, ethnicity
or age, is in itself a tactic to avert the invisible violence which
created the inequalities and injustices suffered by the communities
represented in the first place. The practice of 'socially engaged art'
is rooted in this notion, falsely suggesting that there is scope for
work that isn't subject to neoliberal forces and that the provision
of public funding places cultural producers outside of the market.
It acted as a pacifying tactic for artists who, for a brief moment
in the the 2000s, enjoyed a relatively easy flow of capital from

SHIRI SHALMY &
ANDREA LUKA ZIMMERMAN

state to studio and to publicly-funded galleries, museums and festivals. Many of us with access to art funding happily bought into it, busily recorded 'instances of participation' and proudly reported the number of ethnic minorities who participated in our projects. This particular form of optimism, like cheap perfume, was, for a long time, used to mask the stench of growing financial inequalities, the privatisation of public institutions, the erosion of social housing and the threat to human rights, backed by state mandated police violence and racist borders.

This practice inevitably instrumentalises participants towards a spectacle of inclusion, suggesting that, through the act of taking part, they can together achieve measurable public benefit, within a set of criteria mapped by the funder. As a practitioner working in that era, I remember a strong sense of working towards eligibility, ticking boxes as we went along.

And while people from marginalised communities had to be included as participants or audience members (in order to secure funding), it was the artist's ultimate responsibility to drive the piece and evidence its success. In true neoliberal fashion, the illusion of participation (which can also be called 'social democracy'), quickly narrowed down to an individual and their regulated relationship with a state bureaucracy which, in turn, instrumentalised them too, in order to reproduce, on a bigger scale, the very same illusion.

It was in this context, and my growing opposition to it, that I became interested in Bekki's work. Her plan was painfully simple: recording testimonies by homeless people and playing them back in doorways around the city, in spaces which could have been, but aren't, used for rough sleeping.

It was of immense importance for Bekki that her own voice as the artist and the author of the piece would recede to the background as much as possible and make room for the voices of the people she interviewed. That the piece was distributed, decentralised, dispersed to the point that the disparate elements, while representing parts of a whole, were held together by a feeling, by a memory, rather than the physical constraint of a time or a space. That they were out of the gallery, on the streets.

We discussed, at length, how important it was to position the work outside of the category of socially engaged practice, how it would speak in many voices at once, yet each autonomous and singular. How it was artwork that was pushed so far to the outer reaches of what is considered to be art, that most who came across it would consider it, instead, a part of life. Not a reflection but an action.

TWO REFLECTIONS ON ART
AND NEOLIBERALISM

The motivation behind the piece, as I understood it, was to suggest and experiment with a different kind of practice. To use the 'legitimacy' of art in order to force a narrative into public consciousness, rather than by legitimising the practice through a supposed community benefit, the operating mechanism of Socially Engaged Practice. Homelessness was there before the artwork had been conceived—in Bekki's own experience and in other people's lives. By framing the subject as art, the project dragged the story out of the shadows, sometimes antagonistic and confrontational, but most often quietly defiant—and left it out there, in the city. Framed as art it could speak to a middle class (yet still on the margins of the art world), making it, in a way, easier for people to engage with but not taking away anything of the urgency and the pain.

The project swaps around the usual social roles by creating a platform through which those who are always object-ified and silenced regain their agency: speaking in their own voice, reclaiming space, framing the discourse. But there is no conversation. There is no room for the audience to answer back and 'participate'—they have to listen closely, confined to a space marked by another human's voice.

By the time they stand quietly and listen, the piece has already pulled them off their track. The unannounced voice of a stranger makes them stop mid pace, often turn back on their heels, to locate the sound, to step aside, enter an uncomfortable space between the public and the private and spend an unknown length of time with the voice-ghost of a person they don't know and, in most circumstances, actively avoid.

And while presenting a complete narrative, recorded and edited, levelled and mastered, this is no Hollywood drama. The viewers are not passive consumers. They are activated through occupying the space of a homeless person, through having to consider their relationship to the physical doorway they're in and the voice speaking to them.

Despite this flipping of the usual power dynamics between the homeless and the housed, The Doorways Project carved a space for empathy and solidarity. By relinquishing a privilege, audience members agreed to accept the terms set up by the interviewees. They entered into a contract with the piece, for the length of a few minutes.

The Doorways Project is 'taking sides' by setting out to challenge the normalisation of violence against marginalised people, not as a superficial act of municipal window dressing. It is an act against vanishing. Homeless people already experience the

SHIRI SHALMY &
ANDREA LUKA ZIMMERMAN

ultimate level of exclusion and they are being further displaced by the forces of neoliberalism, gentrification and austerity, which are described elsewhere in this book. The Doorways Project aims to bring their voices back to the gentrified spaces they once occupied and have been banished from. The disembodied voices in doorways were a reminder of their existence and a confrontation against their silencing and removal, against the 'hostile environment', 'sterile spaces', 'hygienic governmentality'.

Unlike many developer-sanctioned works, which pop up in gentrified areas, The Doorways Project doesn't romanticise the people it documents, with the aim of keeping them frozen in an idealised community space-time. It humanises them against the constant attack on their humanity. It doesn't celebrate homelessness — homelessness remains the core horror of the narrative — but speaks about its brutality and points to the ideology that created and sustains it: capitalism.

PERSONA (NON) GRATA: READING THE HUMAN IN THE 'HOMELESS'
·
ANDREA LUKA ZIMMERMAN

The poverty of our century is unlike that of any other. It is not, as poverty was before, the result of natural scarcity, but of a set of priorities imposed upon the rest of the world by the rich. Consequently, the modern poor are not pitied ... but written off as trash. The twentieth-century consumer economy has produced the first culture for which a beggar is a reminder of nothing.[1]

Person (n.): early 13c., from Old French *persone* 'human being, anyone, person' and directly from Latin *persona* 'human being, person, personage; a part in a drama, assumed character', originally 'a mask, a false face', such as those of wood or clay worn by the actors in later Roman theater. In legal use, 'corporate body or corporation having legal rights', 15c. *In person* 'by bodily presence' is from the 1560s.

That John Berger's insightful analysis above feels palpably true can be seen in the many ways in which a dehumanising process has become persuasive across our society — be it in the ubiquity

TWO REFLECTIONS ON ART
AND NEOLIBERALISM

of private security personnel, demanding that 'homeless' (-looking) people move on from park benches and other (privatised) public-appearing spaces; in the use of homeless spikes, in 'donor-friendly' barcodes to be worn around the neck, and in even more experimental measures like the deployment of off-putting atonal music on the S-Bahn in Berlin to deter extended journeys.

The individual, or person, has been taken out of the homeless and has become one of 'the homeless'. We should know from history what dangers lurk in such a process of rendering people into pejorative problems, or even victims. As in Kafka's *Parable Before the Law*, such a 'label' erases the individual circumstances of that human being, with all the memories and pasts and thoughts that make them, for they are now defined and bound by the structures of bureaucracy ostensibly set up to protect, yet which in practice so exclude. These very systems, rendering invisible the hyper-visible, are part of what can be called 'structural violence', and are further heightened because of the ongoing processes of constant erasure faced by the said person in their journey further through the administration of their condition, and the increasingly hopeless, often impossible, attempts to seek redress for, or redirection of, their situation.

Culture claims its own narrative about homelessness. The fact of being or having been homeless becomes part of the overt definition of a person. Culture (made predominantly by people of privilege, be it of class, gender or race) more frequently interrogates people from deprived backgrounds instead of people who hold privilege.

I first came across Bekki's Doorways Project several years ago. Bekki was in the process of developing a larger-scale outdoor sound installation that would tour the country. Bekki's work touched me on such a profound level that when, as part of Fugitive Images, I co-curated a six-week exhibition on housing activism called 'Real Estates' at Peer Gallery in 2015, a work-in-progress installation version of The Doorways Project became a key part of it.

In Bekki's work, life and art are inseparable. Life comes first. Art comes from life. Artists making work about their own life experiences are many, at worst because ours is a world made up of an excessive individual need for validation and recognition. Works about others' experiences are also numerous; when there is a great disjuncture between maker and subject, often around the parameters mentioned above, those lives portrayed can all

SHIRI SHALMY &
ANDREA LUKA ZIMMERMAN

too easily become engines for the imagination and agenda
of the makers (well-intentioned or otherwise), at the expense
of those depicted.

I am not suggesting here that authentic works can only
be made by those who have experienced the situations represented.
This very idea has so often become an excuse for a further silencing
by means of aesthetic or logistical barriers. Yet the questions
remain: who tells (or is allowed to tell), how is the story told, and
for whom? So, on the one hand there is the individual expression
of an experience, and on the other its relation to the larger socio-
political context, one that allows some to thrive, while silencing,
even erasing, others. This latter may not be a conscious or
deliberate act but it is a by-product of our current value system,
one which reduces certain bodies and expressions within the
context of structural violence or a 'pervasive social inequality ...
ultimately backed up by the threat of physical harm',[2] as you will
read in this book.

Some works forget to include the one who is listening,
reading, touching, looking. The Doorways Project allows us
to stop, consider, remain and become part of the work by taking
its stories from and back into the world, where similar stories
can be found on nearly every street corner, waiting to be seen,
heard, acknowledged, witnessed. The Doorways Project renders
experience in place and time as a wound, and at the same time
moves beyond the intimate, singular 'now' of their telling into a
deeper understanding of humans suffering within the mainstream
narratives of a society all too readily tolerating the injustice
of their condition.

Art can both illuminate and erase. This book is about
Bekki's art, and the women within it and beyond who shared with
us such a fundamental part of their lives. So frequently they know
what they need but are told by agents of more or less well-meaning
social and political structures that they actually need something
else. This is no more apparent than in the visual essay comprised
of a selection of letters about Lisa (p. 110), written between
various mental health and housing departments over the course
of a decade. Like the other women here, Lisa knew what help she
required to deal with the extreme trauma she had experienced, but
was either ignored or told repeatedly that she was asking too
much, she was needing too much—that she would need to accept
their offer or none at all.

The way in which mental health is described in official
narratives (as a priority concern, that everyone has access, and
so on) brings to mind the observation of the late Umberto Eco

TWO REFLECTIONS ON ART
AND NEOLIBERALISM

that the same words used in a sentence can mean the opposite. The mental health system is failing traumatised women (as well as many others), and what part does culture play in this? What strategies legitimise this enabling of rejection of the needs of people, allowing them to be 'othered' and pathologised? Cultural production is pervasive in its reach, in its shaping of response, while unthinking and unfeeling bureaucracy enables passivity.

'The sad truth is that most evil is done by people who never make up their minds to be good or evil.'[3] The Doorways Project claims the space within culture that does these things and inserts instead human beings with all their complexity, able to tell their stories of survival, to resist the desertification of life within neoliberal cities.

Home and the absence thereof. It is more than housing that needs to be addressed to shape a world we may be able to live in, regardless of means. We find ourselves in a time where the myth of individualised action and the normalising idea of progress through self-development are dominant. But we cannot genuinely move forward in isolation from each other — or are we now indeed existing in a space where we have learnt to mask 'othering' in a way that appears benevolent? Where cultural annihilation precedes the unspeakable?

'The purpose of the mouse is not to evade the cat. The purpose of the mouse is to exist.'[4] Bekki's work challenges profoundly an unthinking, collective belief in an easy, universal progress. What purpose do pity and charity serve if not the conscience of the perpetrator whose crime will never be judged? Who and what is responsible for the despair of others? We know, but we must become much more aware of the mechanisms by which passivity, apathy and emotional fatigue in the face of such inadequate structures prevail, is even encouraged and, dare we say, desired. The Doorways Project opens onto a shared, aware and active space where this process might begin.

1 JOHN BERGER, *Keeping a Rendezvous* (New York: Pantheon Books, 1991).
2 DAVID GRAEBER, *The Utopia of Rules: On Technology, Stupidity, and the Secret Joys of Bureaucracy* (New York: Melville House, 2015).
3 HANNAH ARENDT, *The Life of the Mind: Volume 1, Thinking* (New York: Harcourt Brace Jovanovich, 1978).
4 KEN APPOLLO, *Humble Works and Mad Wanderings: Street Life in the Machine Age* (Nevada City: Carl Mautz Publishing, 1997).

SHIRI SHALMY &
ANDREA LUKA ZIMMERMAN

THE AFTERMATH OF
STREET HOMELESSNESS
BEKKI PERRIMAN

Home? What does home look like and what does home mean?
It feels like I've survived a hurricane and been caught up for
so long in the eye of the storm, but now it's passed and the sky
is calm and I look around me and it's absolute devastation.
Everything has been knocked down, there is debris everywhere
and how do I begin to pick up the pieces and start to rebuild a
kind of normality? This is what the aftermath of being homeless
feels like, even years later—I feel like I am looking around
at devastation and feeling guilty for being one of the ones who
survived when so many of my close friends didn't make it. Several
of my friends died of heroin overdoses, a couple were murdered
on the street—it is a brutality and violence that is unimaginable
until it becomes your reality every day.

The brutality and violence runs so deep—it is the core
of how being homeless was for me. I remember feeling so invisible
and far removed from the rest of society. Every single day someone
walking past would abuse me—spit on me, tell me to get a job, or
offer me money to sell my body. It was an experience of constantly
being judged, looked down upon and made to feel like I was
worthless and dirty. Those feelings started to become how I felt
about myself, I couldn't shake them off. There came a point when
all my resilience failed and I became completely entrenched in this
lifestyle that I hated but had me gripped in its stranglehold. I want
to try and put into words what it is like to try and leave that behind.

Being housed was never as simple as having a roof over
my head. For a long time I was in and out of many different
hostels and temporary accommodation but I always went back
to the streets. Part of it was about personal safety: I felt too unsafe
indoors where in the hostels it would kick off unexpectedly and
I'd feel cornered and trapped. They weren't safe places to live.
There were needles left on the bathroom floor and blood splashed
up the wall; the atmosphere was angry and aggressive and the staff
mostly left us alone and didn't interact with any of the residents
staying there. To put a lot of traumatised people all under the same
roof, in cramped overcrowded conditions and with no support,
is a recipe for trouble and it brewed through the course of a day
and at night became explosive. I felt safer on the street. On the
streets I could choose where I would sleep and the people I wanted
to be with.

There are many things that kept pulling me back to street
life. I felt a sense of belonging and community on the streets. We
looked out for each other and protected each other and became
like a family. Coming off the streets is a very lonely experience.

BEKKI PERRIMAN

But it wasn't a safe place to be and for as many people as there were who I felt kinship with, there were just as many dangerous, violent types who would steal anything I owned and, being a young girl, I experienced repeated incidents of sexual assault. My situation made me so vulnerable — there was literally no safe place to go. Sadly, I think it's a reality for many young girls on the street that rape and violence just become part of the everyday. I remember going into a day centre, covered in bruises. One of the staff took me aside and asked me what had happened. I told her and that morning she found me fresh clothes and some shoes to wear. She stood outside while I showered and tried to wash away the contamination and the shame. But we never spoke about it again. I had to just pick up the pieces and carry on.

The impact of all this feels like it bore into my soul until I could no longer keep it together anymore. I started to fragment and split off, dissociate, as it was the only way I could survive the painful memories. Trying to come off the streets, you are battling with this feeling of having a reality that is so far from most people's experience. Day to day was about survival and even in the safety of a new home, the horror of memories continued to engulf me. I didn't know how to distance myself from the things I experienced and what I witnessed on the street.

I've found it really difficult to get help for the trauma I've experienced. There is a two-year-long waiting list to access the Post-traumatic Stress Service (one year's wait for an assessment and another year's wait for treatment — that is, if funding is approved) and it is uncertain whether, as a survivor of rape and abuse, I can even access treatment there. For veterans coming back from war zones there is, rightly, PTSD support, but for women who've experienced street homelessness and multiple rape and abuse, what support is out there? My experience has been one of being silenced, being labelled as mentally ill and with that label silenced further, as the symptoms I experience must just be a result of disorder rather than what has happened to me.

It feels like these are things that people don't want to hear. They don't want to hear about childhood abuse, or rape, or domestic violence. They don't want to hear about pain so deep, so raw, that a person might turn to drugs to block it all out. It is easier to blame and stigmatise the women sleeping in doorways than it is to offer them help.

THE AFTERMATH OF
STREET HOMELESSNESS

AFTERWORD
KATE TEMPEST

DOORWAYS

From pillar to post, the ghosts at the edge of the frame
Don't acknowledge them.
You'll only encourage them.
The rain belts down like punishment.
Today was murder.
Tomorrow's just more of the same.

Safer to blank them. *I dragged myself up! I had nothing.*
Says black-eyed barmaid, smoking,
I never begged help off no-one.
Convinced of this
And other convenient lies.
See her fucking trainers?
They were nicer than mine

Closing time
Three tanked-up suits
Arc their piss.
Aim for the head.
Drop fags on her
Offer her money for sex
Youtube in the taxi.
Sleep and forget

She boards the morning train
Of exhausted people with city-sick spirits
And somehow, after the night she's had,
Musters the courage to ask for help –

I know you've all heard it before
And I hate to disturb you ladies and gents /
Fifty grey faces turn back to their phones.
It takes such fucking strength.

The old incantation rings out like a bell
My life's hard enough,
I can't take yours as well

KATE TEMPEST

NOTE ON CONTRIBUTORS

LAURA E. FISCHER

is an interdisciplinary artist, mental health activist and researcher. Her work blends scientific methods with creative approaches and focuses on trauma and the socio-cultural context of violence. She aims to challenge societal constructs, create space for the voices of trauma survivors, research the use of creativity and movement as a body-to-brain approach to healing trauma, and improve our approach to treatment. Laura is an Improvement Leader Fellow of the National Institute for Health Research, has an MSc in Creative Arts and Mental Health, and has worked, exhibited and presented internationally.

ANDREA GIBBONS

is a writer, editor and researcher with over ten years' experience in the US and the UK as a popular educator and community organiser on environmental and economic justice issues. An urban planner and geographer, she is currently part of the Sustainable Housing and Urban Studies Unit (SHUSU) at the University of Salford on housing, homelessness and health, with an interest in social movement and the everyday ways that people work to shape their lives and environments at the intersections of race, class and gender. Her book *City of Segregation: 100 Years of Struggle for Just Housing in Los Angeles*, was published by Verso in 2018.

JANNA GRAHAM

is an organiser, educator and writer committed to practices of radical pedagogy, listening and research. For many years she worked in art galleries as a curator developing projects with communities in struggle around issues of colonialism, racism and the inequalities of urban development. From 2009–14, with Amal Khalaf and others she ran the Centre for Possible Studies, an artist residency and popular education and research centre in London's Edgware Road neighbourhood, supported by the Serpentine Gallery. She is currently a lecturer at Goldsmiths, University of London, a member of the international sound art and political collective Ultra-red and part of the Precarious Workers Brigade.

PIPPA HOCKTON

grew up in Manchester and Birmingham. She trained in psychotherapy at the Lincoln Institute of Psychotherapy in London and has a masters degree in psychodynamic counselling from the University of Birmingham. She practiced in prisons and the NHS before setting up Street Talk in 2006. Street Talk is an outreach therapy service for women in street prostitution and women who have escaped from traffickers. She is a single mother with a son, a daughter and a cat.

ANNA MINTON

is Reader in Architecture at the University of East London and author of *Ground Control: Fear and Happiness in the Twenty-first Century City* (2009) and *Big Capital: Who is London for?* (2017).

MARY PATERSON

is a writer and artist who works collaboratively. Along with Maddy Costa and Diana Damian Martin, she runs Something Other and The Department of Feminist Conversations, two projects that think about the politics of performance, and the performance of politics.

MOYRA PERALTA

octogenarian, FRPS and author of *Nearly Invisible* (2001) — an expression of three decades' involvement documenting aspects of London homelessness — is and has always been a photographer. Over the decades, her numerous occupations have often had other titles: photographer's assistant; wife, mother, nana; dental nurse; receptionist; primary school art teacher; editorial assistant; tutor of adult literacy and photography; night shelter care worker and soup run volunteer; freelance and street photographer; adopter of canines; vocal opponent of prescription medications; and now full-time carer for her spouse. Be that as it may, her occupational knowledge is still empathy and, with her camera never far from hand, she still 'hears things through her eyes'. John Berger paraphrased this well by saying: 'We overhear, with our eyes, two or more voices talking to one another.'

BEKKI PERRIMAN

is an artist interested in creating work around homelessness and mental health. The Doorways Project was commissioned by Unlimited (2016) and is a touring site-specific sound installation exploring homeless culture. Inspired by her experience of life on the streets, Bekki's direct and unsentimental approach investigates the personal, social and political dimensions of homelessness. Through a series of recorded monologues, audiences were invited to intimately engage with the difficult (and mostly ignored) experience of homelessness, and hear first hand the challenges it presents. The Doorways Project was the starting point for this book.

LISA RAFTERY

has had a seventeen-year public and voluntary sector career which has included policy and grant making and the development and delivery of voluntary sector capacity building programmes. She has worked at Homeless Link for the past six years and leads their work on women's homelessness. Lisa is an active campaigner for women's rights and is passionate about supporting women experiencing homelessness through gender- and trauma-informed coordinated services.

SHIRI SHALMY

is a cultural worker and organiser. Over the years she has curated and produced a large number of public art exhibitions and projects, as well as work around radical education and organised labour. She is particularly interested in developing autonomous, self-organised structures around class politics and in movement building through direct action. She is a co-founder of Antiuniversity Now and an organiser with the grassroots campaigning trade union United Voices of the World.

DOORWAYS

ANDREA LUKA ZIMMERMAN

is an artist, film maker and cultural activist, exploring the intersection between public and private memory, in particular in relation to structural and political violence. She grew up on a large council estate, left school at sixteen and later studied through to PhD at Central St. Martins, where she is now a Reader. Andrea's films have been nominated for the Grierson Award, Aesthetica Art Prize, Golden Orange, Jarman Award and Glashuette Documentary Award at the Berlin Film Festival. Recent exhibitions include 'Civil Rites' at the Whitechapel Gallery London Open and Tyneside Cinema Gallery; 'Common Ground' at Spike Island; 'Real Estates' (co-curated with David Roberts) at PEER with LUX, and 'I am here', an architectural photographic installation across the facade of Haggerston estate in Hackney. Feature-length works include *Erase and Forget* (2017); *Estate, a Reverie* (2015) and *Taskafa, Stories of the Street* (2013). Andrea is the co-founder of Vision Machine and the artists' collective Fugitive Images, as well as the winner of the Artangel Open Award 2014 for the forthcoming film *Cycle* with Adrian Jackson (Cardboard Citizens).

EPILOGUE
BEKKI PERRIMAN

While trying to write the closing summary of this book I've been staring at the screen for hours with tears of frustration because I can't find the words to say what I want to say. I can't put into words the sadness, anger, heartbreak and outrage at the injustice of things I've seen throughout my research: women sleeping in industrial waste bins; in abandoned buildings, cemeteries, parks, shop doorways; women sleeping in cars; in 24-hour cafes; on chairs in the waiting room of A&E until they are noticed and kicked out by security.

I've spent hours speaking to women across the UK and listening to their stories. Stories that were told to me with the knowledge they'd be shared publicly in this book, and then the stories which were told to me in confidence which I'll never share because it's not my place to do so. There was an unspoken connection of shared experience. I'd kept my own experience of homelessness bottled up for so long and at times this process has nearly broken me, but the beautiful connections with other women who've experienced homelessness have also held me together. The stories of the women I met on the streets will stay with me forever.

This book is dedicated to Arna who recently died on the streets. I am absolutely devastated that at the end of writing this she is no longer with us.

On a given night it is estimated by official statistics that 4,751 people are sleeping rough in the UK.[1] Last year 449 people died homeless.[2] The average life expectancy of homeless people is just 47 years old, 30 years younger than the national average.[3]

Too many lives are lost on the street. No one should die homeless.

1 Statistics taken from the annual street count, which provides a one-night snapshot of the numbers of people sleeping rough. These figures are likely to be hugely underestimated. Further information can be found via Homeless Link at www.homeless.org.uk/facts/homelessness-in-numbers/rough-sleeping/rough-sleeping-our-analysis.
2 '"A National Scandal": 449 People Died Homeless in the Last Year', *The Bureau of Investigative Journalism* (8 October 2018), available at www.thebureauinvestigates.com/stories/2018-10-08/homelessness-a-national-scandal.
3 'Facts About Homelessness', *The Connection at St Martin's*, available at www.connection-at-stmartins.org.uk/facts-about-homelessness, accessed 5 February 2019.

ABOUT HOUSE SPARROW PRESS

Formed in 2016 to publish *A Sparrow's Journey: John Berger reads Andrey Platonov*, House Sparrow Press is, in the best and multiple senses of the word (it is hoped) an 'occasional' venture. Based in Hackney, London, it seeks to publish creatively committed, collaborative works both at a time that is relevant and for reasons that feel compelling. It is drawn to manuscripts of hybridity, titles that might elude conventional publication over concerns of form or scale. It also believes in a modesty of style (but never of ambition) and a fecundity of ideas. Its moniker (drawn from its first venture) celebrates a creature that was once ubiquitous and yet is now threatened. The idea of a bird inhabiting and inspiring a place of residence also feels resonant. This is what the best books do too. There are wings at work here. In short, Emily Dickinson was right (again) when she observed that 'hope is the thing with feathers'.

House Sparrow Press comprises JESS CHANDLER (Publisher and Editor) and GARETH EVANS (Editor).

DOORWAYS
    WOMEN, HOMELESSNESS,
    TRAUMA AND RESISTANCE
    Photographs, Essays, Interviews

    edited by Jess Chandler, Bekki Perriman,
    Shiri Shalmy, Andrea Luka Zimmerman

Published in 2019 in an edition of 600 copies by
House Sparrow Press, Hackney, London, England
www.housesparrowpress.com

Edition copyright © House Sparrow Press 2019
Text copyright © the individual authors 2019

The moral right of the writers named to be identified as the authors
of their work has been asserted in accordance with the Copyrights,
Designs and Patents Act of 1988. All rights reserved.

Designed by Hannah Ellis. Printed in the UK by Aldgate Press.

No part of this publication may be reproduced, stored in
a retrieval system, or transported in any form by any means,
electronic, mechanical, photocopying, recording or otherwise,
without the prior permission in writing of both the copyright
holders and the above publisher of this book.

ISBN: 978-1-9998161-1-7

A CIP catalogue record for this book is available
from the British Library.

Commissioned and supported by Unlimited, celebrating the work
of disabled artists, with funding from Arts Council England.

SUPPORTED BY